# ATTACK

## ON

# ORLEANS

## THE WORLD WAR I
## SUBMARINE RAID ON CAPE COD

### JAKE KLIM

THE
History
PRESS

*This book is dedicated to Eric Lingard.*

Published by The History Press
Charleston, SC 29403
www.historypress.net

First published 2014
Second printing 2014
Third printing 2015

Manufactured in the United States

ISBN 978.1.62619.490.8

Library of Congress Cataloging-in-Publication Data

Klim, Jake.
Attack on Orleans : the World War I submarine raid on Cape Cod / Jake Klim.
pages cm
Includes bibliographical references and index.
ISBN 978-1-62619-490-8
1. World War, 1914-1918--Massachusetts--Orleans (Town) 2. World War,
1914-1918--Naval operations--Submarine. 3. World War, 1914-1918--Naval operations,
German. 4. Orleans (Mass. : Town)--History, Naval--20th century. 5. Cape Cod (Mass.)--
History, Naval--20th century. I. Title.
D570.85.M41O745 2014
940.4'514--dc23
2014017445

# CONTENTS

# ACKNOWLEDGEMENTS

First, this book would never have come to fruition without the help and support of the Orleans Historical Society (OHS) and its dedicated director, Tamsen Cornell. The OHS graciously provided photos, newspaper articles and firsthand accounts from eyewitnesses, most of which was recorded years before I was born.

William Quinn, Cape Cod's unofficial shipwreck historian and guru of all things Orleans, was a wealth of information and also provided his collection of historic photos for use in this book. Sadly, Mr. Quinn passed away shortly before this book was published. With his passing, Cape Cod lost a great historian.

Glenn Stockwell, Richard Boonistar and Richard Ryder were always willing to lend their expertise on matters relating to Cape Cod's Lifesaving Service, and I thank them for that.

I would also like to thank the following archives and libraries for answering questions, providing insight and supplying photographs: the U.S. Coast Guard Historian's Office; the Gloucester Lyceum & Sawyer Free Library; the U.S. Coast Guard Academy; the W.B. Nickerson Cape Cod History Archives; the Middlesex School; the Cape Cod National Seashore; the Gloucester City Archives; the Cape Ann Museum; the National Archives in Washington, D.C.; the German U-boat Museum and Archive; and NausetHeights.org.

Cheryl Pierce Clarkin, whose great-grandfather Robert Pierce was the keeper at Station Number 40 in Orleans, provided information and photographs about her relative. Likewise, Stephen Hopkins, the son of

# ACKNOWLEDGEMENTS

Reuben Hopkins, one of the surfmen involved in the rescue, was gracious to supply a photo and information about his father.

Thanks to Jonathon Amato for translating German documents, to Chuck Kacsur for producing the maps and graphics and to Shannon O'Neill for her legal counsel.

Susan Downman, a distant relative of Eric Lingard, contacted me after this book was published and passed along information, previously unknown to me, for this updated edition.

I would also like to thank the numerous friends and colleagues who read drafts of my chapters and provided their feedback and assisted in the acquisition of articles and literature: Peter Silverman, Katherine Mischenko, Bert Rodriguez, Dianne Langeland, Dr. Clayton Laurie, Emily Norton, Jenny Curtis, Katie Andreassi, Brian Leonard, Will Fink, Christiam Camacho, Suran De Silva, Brian Knowlton, Suzanne Mullin Koppanen, Shaun Johnson, Jordan Snyder and Jessi Steward.

Finally, I need to thank my family—my parents, Jack and Cathy, and my sister, Kate—for their love and support.

# INTRODUCTION

The dorsal fin, which broke the surface just fifteen feet off Nauset Beach in Orleans, was indeed an ominous sight. The great white shark, estimated to measure twelve to fifteen feet long, was casually making its way along the arm of Cape Cod, Massachusetts. On shore, hundreds of beachgoers, mouths agape, pointed and stared. Many were in the midst of their summer vacations, and the spectacle before them was unlike anything they had ever seen before. Due to the increased number of sightings, town officials barred sunbathers from entering the ocean, but ironically, these warnings did little to dissuade the curious from descending toward the water's edge.

Nearly one hundred years earlier, on a hot, hazy morning during the summer of 1918, a similar crowd gathered at Nauset Beach. Although it was three miles offshore, the "big tin whale," as it was described by one witness, was over two hundred feet in length and visible to everyone on the beach. Like the great white shark, its presence so close to shore was disconcerting, but bystanders could not look away. Instead, like a magnet, the leviathan attracted the attention of upward of one thousand curious onlookers.

Today, high above the beach, nestled in the bluff, a modest sign marks the occasion:

> *Three miles offshore, in the direction of the arrow, was the scene of attack of a German submarine on a tug and barges July 21, 1918. Several shells struck the beach. This is the only section of the United States' coast shelled by the enemy during World War I.*

Historical sign above Nauset Beach. *Courtesy of Joe Navas/Organic Photography.*

Despite the best efforts of the kind-hearted citizens who erected the sign, it is essentially invisible to those sunbathing on the beach below. In fact, the marker is located on a private stairwell. To the countless throngs who frequent Nauset Beach on any given summer day, what happened here during the last summer of the First World War remains largely unknown, despite the event's historical significance.

What follows is the true story of an interesting and forgotten anecdote in American history known as the Attack on Orleans. It is also a story about two first responders and the roles their respective outfits played during the attack. One was a native Cape Codder—a seaman from another era, born a year after the end of the Civil War—who was destined to make his living off the sea. The other was an ambitious young man, not yet thirty years old, born into a life of privilege and who eventually found his way into the cockpit of a seaplane. Finally, this is a story about the small town of Orleans, which sits on the "elbow" of Cape Cod, ever geographically vulnerable to threats from the sea.

# CHAPTER 1

# A SURFMAN NAMED PIERCE

*The life saver's work is always arduous, often terrible.*
—*John W. Dalton*

The town of Orleans is located on the "elbow" of Cape Cod, which resembles a flexed arm protruding into the Atlantic Ocean. Like the sands on its beaches, the borders have shifted over the years, but today, Orleans encompasses approximately twenty-one square miles, one-third of which touches salt water. The small coastal hamlet is squeezed between Cape Cod Bay to the west and the vast Atlantic Ocean to the east, which splashes against Nauset Beach, a ten-mile expanse that extends south to neighboring Chatham. Pleasant Bay rests to the south of Orleans, giving the town a curious shape, as if that part of it has slowly been eroded by the sea over time. The town is peppered with saltwater ponds and littered with geographical features like necks, points and narrows. Countless coves, rivers and marshes rise and drain with the daily floods, giving the air the taste of salt and the smell of tide.

From autumn to spring, the town is a quiet place to visit, but in the summer, like the rest of the Cape, the population of Orleans nearly triples. In July and August, thousands of tourists from Boston, located nearly ninety miles away, and other urban centers take to the narrow, sandy roads that meander like tentacles to the various cottages and vacation homes burrowed among Orleans' bluffs. Once there, tourists descend on the town's pristine beaches, where they fish, surf, harvest shellfish or simply relax in the sand.

Southern New England. *Chuck Kaesur.*

Orleans' small-town charm has been welcoming people for centuries. Pilgrims seeking additional land and fertile soil settled in Orleans just before the start of the eighteenth century. However, it would be another one hundred years before the town was incorporated and named after Louis Phillipe II, the Duke of Orleans, allegedly in recognition for French support during the American Revolution. Early settlers cut down trees to clear land for farms and pastures and used that timber to build and heat their homes—and to construct ships. Throughout these growing pains, Nauset Indians and English settlers coexisted peacefully. The Indians even went so far as to teach the colonists how to harvest shellfish, which proved to be a dependable source of food and income for those who mastered the craft.

Others took to the business of salt, which was needed to preserve the vast quantities of fish that arrived from the sea each day. In order to fill this need, saltworks—buildings that produced salt—were constructed throughout the town. They would go on to gain great fame in Orleans and throughout Cape Cod at the beginning of the nineteenth century as salt-making quickly became an extremely lucrative enterprise. As a result, the prevalent industry would eventually find itself in the crosshairs when hostilities broke out between the British and the Americans on Cape Cod during the War of 1812.

On December 12, 1814, Britain's HMS *Newcastle* ran aground on a shoal off the coast of Orleans. In an effort to lighten the ship's load and shift it off the sand bar, British sailors tossed some of the ship's items overboard, which were, in turn, salvaged by "beachcombers"—local residents who roamed the shores after wrecks in search of goods and treasure. When word reached the British that American vagabonds had ransacked their discarded supplies, tempers flared. Armed barges, under the command of Lieutenant Frederick Marryat, were dispatched with orders to reclaim His Majesty's property and to take revenge on the town of Orleans.

Early on the morning of December 19, British troops seized four unarmed American ships, including one loaded with salt from the nearby saltworks, at the mouth of Rock Harbor Creek on the Cape Cod Bay side of Orleans. The next day, Lieutenant Marryat, hungry for more destruction, decided to burn ships, docks and buildings associated with the town's saltworks industry. Without a moment to spare, militiamen from Orleans and neighboring villages arrived on scene and began to lay down heavy musket fire against the marauding redcoats. Lieutenant Marryat was forced to turn tail, but not before eleven of his men were struck down by, as one British officer snarled, "those wretches in Orleans."

The heroics of Cape Cod's militias that historic day became the stuff of legend. For the second time in less than fifty years, Orleanians had helped throw the British back across the Atlantic Ocean. However, it was the Atlantic itself that proved to be the town's greatest adversary.

Orleanians, and especially residents who have lived along Nauset Beach, are no strangers to the howling winds and tumultuous seas that assault the coast. For thousands of years, nature had wreaked havoc on the town's beaches and the bluffs. When storms hit the Cape's coast, they typically come across the Atlantic, from the east. These nor'easters can pack hurricane-force gales and typically cause erosion and coastal flooding. Usually these storms come with rain, but depending on the temperature, they can also bring snow.

Since the first colonists began to arrive by ship in the early seventeenth century, the wicked seas off Cape Cod have claimed thousands of lives. The outer arm of the Cape contains a series of hidden shoals and sandbars, into which mariners have the tendency to run their ships during inclement weather. The combination makes these waters some of the most dangerous on the East Coast and a graveyard for ships and sailors alike. "There is no other part of the world, perhaps," wrote the director of the U.S. Coast and Geodetic Survey in 1869, "where tides of such very small rise and fall are accompanied by such strong currents running far out to sea."

When word of a shipwreck rang through the town—"Ship ashore! All hands perishing!"—the Cape's good-hearted and curious townspeople would flock to the beach in an effort to lend a hand. Despite their good nature, they could do very little from the beach and would watch helplessly as the sea chewed up wooden schooners, sometimes less than a mile from shore. In the days, and sometime hours, after the disaster, beachcombers would walk the length of the shore seeking various riches brought in by the surf—coffee, foodstuffs, wine, tobacco, cotton or spices—and haul them away by hand or horse-drawn cart. If a crew member were fortunate enough to make it to the beach alive, he would be cared for by the locals. However, most times the waves carried the lifeless body of a sailor in from the wreck.

The Massachusetts Humane Society recognized that something had to be done to aid shipwreck victims, and in 1786, it decided to build small, makeshift huts on desolate stretches of Cape Cod's coast. If a victim actually survived a shipwreck and made it to shore, the cold, wet sailor could take shelter in one of these huts instead of freezing to death on the windswept beach. As time went on, these huts grew into larger stations that housed lifeboats. If a storm raged out at sea, quick-thinking volunteers could report to these stations and launch a lifeboat to assist those in peril offshore.

By 1845, Massachusetts boasted eighteen such stations. But despite these resources, shipwrecks and the subsequent loss of life continued to surge. In 1871, a study was commissioned to determine what should be done. The resulting report indicated that the crews who manned these stations lacked discipline, that certain stations were missing vital resources and that the surf stations themselves were badly in need of repair. As it existed, the surf station project was a failure, but it was too important to abandon.

In time, more money was pumped into the stations, station crews were compensated and station keepers—those in charge of the station—who failed at their duty were sacked and replaced with capable officers. It was also decided, as a result of the report, that surfmen, or lifesavers, should patrol between stations, all day and all night in an effort to give the shoreline more of a human presence.

In what is considered the definitive history on Cape Cod's lifesaving service, author John Willfred Dalton described in his book *Life Savers of Cape Cod* how surfmen would spend "hours of racking labor [in] protracted exposure to the roughest weather conditions, and a mental and bodily strain under the spur of exigency and the curb of discipline that exhaust even the hardy fearless coast guardians." These "solitary patrols with great peril" would continue day and night "in moonlight, starlight, thick darkness, driving tempest, wind, rain, snow or hail…an endless line of life savers steadily march along the exposed beaches on the outlook for endangered vessels." Sometimes patrolling surfmen had to hold a wooden shingle in front of their faces to keep sand out of their eyes during such patrols.

The long and often monotonous work of a lifesaver was punctuated by moments of intense danger. If a surfman spotted a vessel in distress during his patrol, he would rush back to his station and rouse the keeper and the other surfmen, and together they would launch one of the station's surfboats into the sea. The water was typically quite cold, and during certain months, it bordered on freezing. Each time a surfman participated in such a rescue, his life was in danger. The trials and tribulations endured by surfmen were more appropriately summed up by their motto: "You have to go, but you don't have to come back."

In 1872, nine new stations were built on Cape Cod, including Station Number 40 in Orleans. The construction of Station Number 40 and others like it could not have come soon enough; by the 1880s, shipwrecks were occurring on the Cape's outer arm at an average of one every two weeks. Tucked back away from the high tide line among the bluffs on Little Pochet Island, Station Number 40 was located approximately five miles from the center of town. The dark red building was comfortable, but it lacked electricity and running water. The first floor had a kitchen, a sitting room, a supply room and an office for the keeper, while the second floor served as a sleeping room for the surfmen and, when circumstances called for it, quarters for rescued sailors. On top of the building, a watchtower jutted into the sky. Here, surfmen could keep a keen eye on the happenings out at sea. By the early twentieth century, Station Number 40 was connected with telephone lines that ran to central stations in Provincetown and Chatham. If a situation were to arise that needed additional attention, the station's keeper could confer with the superior officer in Provincetown or the recently built Chatham Naval Air Station.

Station Number 40 sat on one of the most dangerous sections of Cape Cod's coast. Deadly sandbars offshore constantly kept the station's six to eight surfmen on their toes, so it was imperative to have it manned by good personnel. The men at Station Number 40 were a hardy, disciplined bunch, and throughout the week, they drilled in anticipation for the inevitable

Station Number 40. *From* Life Savers of Cape Cod.

Robert F. Pierce (second from left). *From* Life Savers of Cape Cod.

rescue. In the first thirty years of its existence, the surfmen at the Orleans station had saved well over one hundred lives.

Robert Francis Pierce rose through the ranks of the lifesaving service to become the keeper at Station Number 40. Tall, gangly and balding, fifty-two-year-old "Bert" Pierce might not have looked the part of a seasoned seaman, but the keeper had been around boats his entire life. The son of a Wampanoag Indian, Pierce was a native Cape Codder, born in the small town of Harwich in 1866. He grew up fishing on boats, and it was clear that someday he would make a living off the sea. When he was in his mid-twenties, Pierce pondered which career path to take in life. Working on ships might offer adventure and good wages, but there was something intriguing to Pierce about the lifesaving service. Candidates were required to submit a "vouchers under oath," which proved they had worked a minimum of three years as a sailor or boatman. Applicants also had to be at least five feet, eight inches tall; weigh no more than 190 pounds; and live within five miles of their assigned station. Finally, interested aspirants were required to provide a certificate of physical health that proved they were resilient enough to endure the hardships required of them.

In 1890, Pierce passed the required tests and was assigned as a lifesaver at nearby Monomoy Point Station. While stationed there, twenty-four-year-old Pierce faced "the greatest of dangers" during the numerous rescues that he participated in. According to one report, "[Pierce] was skilled in the art of handling boats in the surf, and took naturally to the work he has been called upon to perform since joining the life-saving service."

In 1898, having spent eight years in the lifesaving service, Pierce, now married and the father of a young child, was transferred to the Old Harbor Life Saving Station in Chatham, where, at the age of thirty-one, he was awarded the position of number one surfman. This title was bestowed upon the highest-ranking surfman, besides the keeper, at any given station.

One day, while on patrol at Old Harbor, Pierce "saw a skiff with a small lad in her who had come out from Chatham for a little fun." The craft ventured out into the current, which apparently became too much for the child to handle. An after-action report written later described how Pierce saved the day:

*Number 1 Surfman Pierce moved the…surfboat and hastened out to where the frail craft was. The lad of 7 years was crying and trying his best to hold his own against the tide. He climbed into the surfboat, and they took the row boat in tow and landed them safe in the harbor where*

Robert F. Pierce and family. *Courtesy of Cheryl Pierce Clarkin.*

*he* [parted] *from a very thankful lad promising never to be caught in such a scrape again.*

On November 6, 1911, Pierce was promoted to the coveted position of keeper and assigned to the Gay Head Life-Saving Station on Martha's Vineyard. A few years later, he was transferred back to the mainland and assigned to other stations, eventually ending up at Station Number 40 in Orleans.

\*\*\*

Throughout the latter part of the nineteenth century, there were rumors that a canal would be built through the isthmus of Cape Cod. Once constructed, captains would have the option to bypass the Cape's formidable "forearm," long susceptible to shipwrecks, and quickly cut through the Cape's "shoulder," a distance of only seven and a half miles. A canal would greatly reduce the time it took mariners to get from Boston to New York or any other points south, but most importantly, it would decrease the likelihood that steamers, schooners and crafts of all sizes might run aground during inclement weather. Without ships to look after, many assumed that the era of the surfman, at least those stationed along the arm of Cape Cod, would inevitably come to an end.

After seven years of construction, the long-awaited Cape Cod Canal was finally completed in 1914. It was a welcomed relief that would save sailors traveling south over one hundred miles. However, this shortcut came with a price—a toll. After spending $12 million on its construction, investors were eager to recuperate their losses. As a result, some shipping companies preferred to go the longer, more treacherous route instead of paying the expensive toll, despite the heightened risks to the sailors on board the crafts.

For the time being, the job of the surfmen, it seemed, was spared.

In the years following the canal's completion, the surfmen of Orleans were on the lookout for something more ominous than bad weather and ships in distress. On February 6, 1918, just two weeks before Pierce took command of Station Number 40, the U.S. Navy convened a special meeting in Washington, D.C., to discuss an impending concern: "Defense against submarine attack in home waters."

The United States had been at war with Germany for almost a year. Although the Zimmerman Telegram ultimately brought the two belligerents to blows, Germany's fleet of submarines had been sinking Allied and neutral ships since 1914, killing American citizens in the process. Germany's *Unterseeboot*, or U-boat, was a horrific yet highly effective weapon of war. But for the most part, the German navy, or *Kaiserliche Marine*, sank ships near Europe, far from American shores. Germany constructed nearly four hundred submarines during the First World War, but only seven were long-range cruisers, capable of sailing from one side of the Atlantic to the other. These "super submarines" were unlike anything the rest of the world had seen before. With a cruising radius of twenty-five thousand miles, they pushed the limits of what submarines were capable of during the war.

Germany's super submarines, the board warned, "may appear in American waters without warning" and "may be used on our coast with a view to divert some of our military activity away from European waters." Specifically, their goal was to disrupt American troop and supply transport, but the board also cautioned that the "bombardment of coastal towns may also be done."

Historically, the Atlantic Ocean had served as a buffer between the United States and Europe, but with the advent and subsequent success of Germany's U-boat during the first four years of the war, an enemy from afar now had the ability to sail west undetected toward American soil. If any of Germany's seven super submarines found their way to the western Atlantic, they could instill fear in the veins of the American populace and rattle the psyche of the U.S. government.

However, the American public was not privy to the information the U.S. Navy had at its disposal. With the Atlantic Ocean serving as a safeguard, Americans remained isolationists; the war against Germany and its allies was being waged in Europe, or, as the famous George M. Cohan war song at the time indicated, "Over There," not over here.

# CHAPTER 2
# A GOOD ENOUGH GOD FOR ME

*When a boy gets into Harvard and the world, he has to stand on his own feet.*
—*Rollin M. Gallagher, Eric Lingard's teacher*

As he ascended the hill he had climbed twice already that day, Eric Lingard's mind began to wander; this was not how he envisioned spending his workday. Downhill, below him, hired hands labored away inside the icehouse he had constructed. The 1,200-ton plant, located on the family's beautiful seaside property—"The Pines"—in the village of Annisquam, Massachusetts, had taken the twenty-four-year-old six weeks to build, and all things considered, it was a successful little venture. Still, working in an icehouse was not what Lingard wanted to be doing at this stage in his life.

One year earlier, the handsome but boyish-looking Lingard was enrolled at Harvard Law School with aspirations of becoming an attorney. Sadly, in 1915, during the middle of his second year, Lingard's mother, Adele, passed away. Adele had been caring for Lingard's younger sister, Olga, who was suffering from illness. Now, without any family to look after her, that job fell to Eric. Throughout the day, Lingard would break away from his icehouse and, sometimes under a warm summer sun, climb the hill that led to his house and visit Olga, hoping to raise her spirits. The hill was steep, but his reward was worth it. He could never visit for very long because he also needed to mind his ice-making business; in addition to managing his workers, Lingard personally handled thirty thousand pounds of ice each day. It was an exhausting endeavor, but Lingard was not one to shy away from hard work.

The early life of Eric Adrian Alfred Lingard is shrouded in mystery. He was allegedly born in the posh Beacon Hill neighborhood of Boston in 1890, though some records suggest he might have been born a year later or in England or Switzerland. He and his sister, Olga, grew up in a big Victorian-style home on a large tract of land alongside Lobster Cove in Annisquam. Brother and sister had the finest of clothes, and their home was outfitted with beautiful furniture imported from afar. Adele, who had summered in famous resorts in various countries, apparently loved the small coastal hamlet because it resembled a Swiss chalet. "This charm has in it the rare combination of sea and land," she noted, "which affords the greatest number of outdoor pastimes and appeals to every mood."

With a thick set of brown hair and dark eyes, a neighbor described the young, freckled Lingard as a "faun—untamed and shy with a smile like sunlight flecking autumn leaves." However, as he grew older and entered secondary school at Middlesex, in the Boston suburb of Concord, the once-innocent Lingard grew somewhat rambunctious and, because of his exploits, accrued numerous infractions. His success at Middlesex was far from ideal, and outside of music, he rarely received good marks in the classroom. Still, Lingard was considered a loyal and devoted friend and was adored

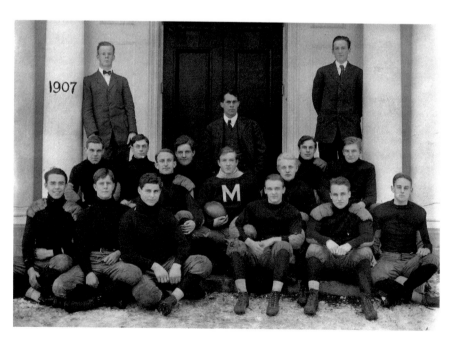

Eric Lingard (seated far left), the Middlesex football star. *Courtesy of the Middlesex School.*

by classmates and teachers alike. One high school pal simply referred to Lingard as "a good enough God for me." Affectionately known as "Muscular Mugs," a result of breaking his nose, Lingard made the football team as a sophomore and played tackle for three years. On the field, he was revered for his "aggressiveness and persistency." By the time he graduated, Lingard had developed into a strong young man with a "fine physique" and was "considered one of the best linemen the school has ever had."

In 1907, seventeen-year-old Eric caught pneumonia and was forced to finish the remainder of his school year without his mother around. Adele Randolph von Liberich, socialite extraordinaire, was in Paris at the time. Adele lived a life of privilege emulated by many and experienced by few. Born in Hungary in 1869, she claimed to be the daughter of an Austro-Hungarian diplomat and allegedly could speak seven languages. She supposedly met her husband, Dr. Henry R. Lingard, in England, and together they immigrated to the United States to start life anew. Although she spent a great deal of time shoring up her social status in Boston's high society, letters suggest that Adele cared deeply about her children, and Eric frequently accompanied her on soirées overseas. During one particular trip to Germany, Eric was able to "inspect" the royal stables at the ambassador's residence, which, Adele boasted, were "among the finest in Europe." Eric's father, Henry, supposedly died in 1908, when Eric was eighteen years old, and shortly thereafter, a wealthy man whom Eric and Olga referred to as "Uncle" became the paternal figure at The Pines; but he was constantly coming and going, having himself settled with another family in the American Midwest. In fact, some records suggest that there had never been a Henry Lingard, and "Uncle" was, and always had been, father, which meant that Adele's entire backstory had been fabricated. Whatever the truth may be, word of her unflattering personal life leaked, and some in her social circles began to describe Adele as a "bigamist" and "mistress"—claims that would later have a negative impact on the family's once-pristine social status.

Despite his poor academic record, and perhaps with the help of his family name, Lingard gained admittance to Harvard, where he continued his football career and earned a letter as a fullback. Physically, Lingard was one of the strongest students at the university. He was also one of the most popular. Following in the footsteps of his mother, Lingard became a member of various social clubs, making additional friends along the way. Upon graduating in 1913, Lingard immediately enrolled in Harvard Law, but he dropped out just two years into the program when his mother passed away and his sister fell ill, at which point he opened his ice-making business. Later

Eric Lingard
(seated far
left), 1908.
*Courtesy of
the Middlesex*
*School.*

that year, "Uncle" also passed away, which left Eric and his sister in dire financial straits. Although they were rumored to receive annual allowances, the Lingard children depended on the Midwesterner's money, so with his passing, their entire lifestyle changed.

Perhaps it was the arduous workload, or perhaps it was the boredom or simply Lingard's willingness to do something for his country, but once America declared its intentions and joined the war in the spring on 1917, Lingard left his ice-making venture and found work as a laborer "building boats to beat the sub" at the Fore River Shipyard in nearby Quincy. Here, for upwards of twelve hours a day, Lingard laboriously helped construct sub-chasers for the U.S. Navy. Sub-chasers were small, fast ships armed with deck guns and depth charges that, as their name suggests, were built to hunt down German submarines. They were built out of wood, not steel, so construction of ships transpired quickly in boat yards like the one in which Lingard worked. The work at the shipyard, as described by Lingard, was "stiffer than ice and football combined," and he longed to sail aboard sub-chasers rather than build them. After spending four months at Fore River, Lingard attempted to enlist in the U.S. Navy because, as Lingard put it, he wanted "more direct action."

"Having spent most of my summers in temperamental speedboats," Lingard said, "I applied for Naval Aviation." However, the waiting list was clogged with like-minded patriots, and he was turned away. To Lingard, the "War was looking darned exclusive."

A friend suggested he instead attempt to enlist in Washington, D.C., which was still soliciting recruits. Lingard took his friend's advice and soon found his way to the nation's capital. On September 12, 1917, Lingard was examined, and twenty-four hours later, the young man from Annisquam was the newest member of the U.S. Navy's fledgling air arm.

"Out of the fight, something must be coming to the world—some real action," explained Lingard shortly after he enlisted. "Whatever that gain is, we'll all share in it. And when that time comes, I'd hate to think some other fellow had done my fighting for me."

Shortly thereafter, Lingard journeyed to Pensacola, Florida, to earn his wings. During practice flights, he was obsessed with making direct hits with bombs. On one particular training exercise, a crew member explained how Lingard "released the bombs, which landed almost in the center of the designated space—which, had it been a sub and the bombs live ones, would have put an end to everything below." Upon graduating, the station's commanding officer gave the aviator an "Above average. Excellent" rating and described Lingard as "calm, even tempered, forceful [and] active."

On March 18, 1918, Lingard, who had now grown fond of smoking enormous cigars, was commissioned an ensign. Now it would be only a matter of time before Lingard was sent overseas to fight Germans in the skies above France. At least, that was what the eager ensign assumed.

***

When America entered the World War* on April 6, 1917, naval aviation was in its infancy. In 1917, the department had just one operating air station, forty-eight aviators and student aviators and fifty-four aircraft at its disposal.

That year, the Joint Army and Navy Board of Aeronautical Cognizance decided to build six new air stations on the East Coast. One of these six stations would be built in Chatham, Massachusetts, just ten miles south of Orleans, on the "elbow" of Cape Cod.

Ground broke on the Chatham Naval Air Station on August 29, 1917, almost five months after America entered the war. The navy constructed the base on a thirty-six-acre tract of land on Nickerson Neck alongside Pleasant Bay, a protected body of water suitable for seaplanes to take off and land.

---

* The First World War was referred to simply as "the World War" prior to the Second World War and is labeled as such throughout this book.

Time was of the essence, and laborers and contractors alike could find good wages working to build an air base from scratch. For the rest of the summer and on into the fall, construction crews at the base hammered away, all while the war raged overseas. While not entirely complete, in October 1917, the American flag was raised at the base in front of a patriotic crowd of several thousand Bay Staters, who came "afoot, by teams and in hundreds of cars."

The first four planes arrived at the air station in crates in late March 1918, but equally important was finding capable aviators to fly them—a difficult task in the early days of aviation. Making matters worse, many of America's top pilots were already in France dueling with Germans in dogfights above the trenches of the western front.

Rear Admiral Spencer S. Wood, the commandant of the First Naval District in Boston and who oversaw the construction of the Chatham Naval Air Station, used what political muscle he had and tried to secure the best and brightest pilots he could for Cape Cod. One particular candidate, a Harvard man and the son of a prominent Boston socialite, caught Wood's eye. In a letter to a cohort in Washington, the commandant wrote, "I have learned that one Ensign Lingard, who has just been commissioned, would be very valuable to the Station because of his professional attainments…If

Phillip B. Eaton (center), 1917. *U.S. Coast Guard.*

you could see your way clear to let us have this man, we would be very glad to get him."

Shortly thereafter, with Wood's prodding, Lingard was sent back to his native Massachusetts and stationed in Chatham "for patrol duty pending foreign orders." However, because Lingard was familiar with the New England coast, his foreign orders were kept perpetually "pending." Resigned to his fate, Lingard was certain he would never see any action, at least not on this side of the Atlantic.

By June, 250 enlisted men had been assigned to Chatham, and Philip B. Eaton took command of the station. A 1908 graduate of the U.S. Coast Guard Academy and one of the first coast guard aviators, Eaton was older and more experienced than some of his counterparts in the navy and was an ideal candidate to run the new air station. Most recently, Eaton had been executive officer at the Montauk Naval Air Station at the eastern tip of Long Island. And upon acquiring the job at Chatham, he was promoted two grades to captain. In addition to serving as the station's commander, Eaton regularly flew patrols in the waters off Cape Cod and, in doing so, honed his skills in case an emergency should ever arise offshore.

Curtiss HS-1L flying boat. *Courtesy of the San Diego Air & Space Museum.*

One week after Eaton's arrival, the Chatham Naval Air Station acquired four new HS-1L "flying boats" from the Curtiss Aeroplane and Motor Corporation plant in Buffalo, New York. Like other naval aircraft of its day, the HS-1L was amphibious and therefore ideal for operations, should any occur, off the shore of Chatham.

The Curtiss HS was a single-engine, pusher-type biplane with an open cockpit. It had a maximum speed of ninety miles per hour but could fly at a cruising speed for about four hours. One pilot described the Curtiss as "a heavy plane...staunchly built, could land in a fairly rough sea when emergency demanded, and could take off in a moderate sea." Many thought the airplane's motor to be the finest manufactured during the entire war. The flying boat required the pilot to be vigilant because it "had to be constantly 'flown' while in the air...If she stalled, she went into a spin." Such a predicament could be disastrous for the pilot and his crew: "No flyer that I've heard of ever pulled a fully manned and equipped HS-2L* out of a spin. Everyone that spun crashed, killing all on board."

Despite being an entire ocean away from the war zone, accidents occurred at the Chatham Naval Air Station, and casualties while training in planes and operating various pieces of equipment were not uncommon. In April 1918, one of Lingard's colleagues, a machinist, was struck in the head by a signal rocket that ricocheted off the water. He was quickly rushed to the air station's hospital but died in the emergency room a few hours later. Three months later, Ensign Junius Andrews and Lieutenant J.K. Parks were flying in their seaplane when it experienced some type of power failure, crashed on the beach and erupted into flames. Andrews died instantly, his body burned beyond recognition, while Parks survived with terrible burns about the face and hands. Needless to say, the life of a pilot in the early days of aviation was not for the faint of heart. Despite these casualties, the business of flying patrols went on unabated. The air station's primary objective was to protect the shipping industry within its designated zone, should Germany decide to unleash any of its super submarines against the American coast. When he arrived, Lingard was one of just eight pilots at the air station. Patrols were flown in pairs from dawn to dusk, and he routinely spent seven to eight hours a day patrolling the skies south of Cape Cod. Whenever possible, there were two additional planes on standby at the air station, should any emergencies arise. If, and when, the air station received an SOS, pilots like Lingard strived to be airborne within seven minutes.

---

* The HS-2L had bigger rudders and a larger wingspan than its predecessor, the HS-1L.

Throughout the spring and into the early summer, Lingard and the other aviators at Chatham continued to train ad nauseam, but frustratingly, few airmen ever got a chance to showcase their talents. Instead, the pilots at Chatham flew countless "sorties" at events like Liberty Loan Drives and other affairs endorsed by the air station. These were more or less air demonstrations for the delight of the general public, special dignitaries and superior officers. Pilots would loop and twist about while audiences below "ooohed" and "ahhhed" in delight. While enjoyable, these courtesy flyovers were not the "action" Lingard and his fellow airmen had in mind when they enlisted in the U.S. Navy. As the summer of 1918 wore on, many pilots at Chatham sensed the war would inevitably be won by the Allies and privately longed to be transferred to air stations in France before the war was over.

The "action" Lingard craved was undoubtedly in Europe, not Cape Cod.

# CHAPTER 3

# A WHALE WITH TEETH

*The Atlantic coast is ideal for enemy submarine operations.*
*—anonymous naval officer, 1918*

In mid-June, during the last summer of the World War, the super submarine *U-156* slipped quietly into the Atlantic. She was about to begin her second cruise, but exactly where she would sail was anyone's guess.

Engineers and builders at the Atlas Werke shipyard in Bremen constructed the *U-156* during the winter of 1916–17, when the war was at its zenith. However, it had not come easy; a harsh winter caused a shortage of coal, and transportation difficulties hindered supplies from reaching shipyards. To add to Germany's trouble, in 1917, low morale was widespread among dockworkers. Despite these circumstances, the *U-156* was launched in April of that year and was bound for, or drawn to, ships off the Iberian Peninsula.

The *U-156* was one of the largest submersibles the German navy had at its disposal. Over two hundred feet in length and measuring almost ten yards at the beam, at sea, the raider resembled an enormous whale. She was painted dark gray and aside from her conning towers was smooth all around. Her sheer size was certainly something to marvel, but this particular whale had teeth; just below the water line, two torpedo tubes protruded from the bow of the ship. However, torpedoes were expensive, and the raider carried only eighteen of these projectiles when she set sail. Topside were two 5.9-inch deck guns—one forward, one aft—capable of threatening any enemy ship smaller than a cruiser. The *U-156* typically could fire her deck gun well beyond the range of her enemy's cannons, which is why these projectiles were so effective. If, and when, the U-boat did run into trouble, she rarely had to submerge because her armament was on an equal or greater footing than that of her adversary.

On the surface, the *U-156* could cruise at twelve knots, but when submerged, her speed dropped to just five. The ship could dive 146 feet, and with a draft of just 17 feet, she had the ability to crawl extremely close to the coast. Two periscopes enabled her to spy on what was happening onshore or on unsuspecting ships that might sail past, while a wireless transmitter connected her to Berlin. Needless to say, the *U-156* was properly outfitted for an expedition far away from the fatherland, but in early 1918, after sinking just nine Allied merchant ships in the waters west of Portugal, the raider returned to Germany and was placed under new command.

When the raider began her second cruise, in mid-June, she was captained by thirty-five-year-old Kapitänleutnant Richard Feldt. "German appearing" with a military presence, Captain Feldt was a stout man who weighed 170 pounds and stood five feet, seven inches tall. However, with handsome blue eyes and a healthy face, Feldt did not resemble the mustachioed, spike-helmeted caricature many Americans had come to familiarize the German military with.

Despite the dire situation back on the western front, morale on board the German raider seemed high. An officer from another super submarine noted how a transatlantic journey was "something on the Jules Verne order," a notion that was likely echoed by the men on the *U-156*. Between fifty-six and seventy-three sailors, ranging in age from twenty to thirty-five, bivouacked in her belly, where they slept on thin mattresses atop wooden lockers. Ventilators were scarce (if they existed at all), and the air, predictably, was extremely foul. The crew was described as being in "good health and condition." Their only visible fault was that they "suffered from lack of vegetables." Naturally, fresh produce was hard to acquire in the middle of the Atlantic. Scurvy, a disease in which the human body lacks sufficient vitamin C, had been haranguing sailors for centuries, and apparently the crew of the *U-156* was not spared. Despite being so far from home, the crew members still ate well, though the quality of their diet was certainly something to debate. The sub's galley was filled with nonperishables, liquors, tobacco products and other foodstuffs that would not spoil. They drank tea and coffee and ate things like bread (which was dark), butter (which was reportedly not very good) and marmalade, all of which came in tin cans. Sugar, if you could get your hands on it, was a coveted commodity.

Captain Feldt spoke limited English, or, as one American ship captain noted, "enough to get by when the circumstances called for it." Several other members of the crew spoke English as well, all with varying degrees of effectiveness, and some even had intimate connections with the United States. Reportedly, one of the officers even owned a summer home in Maine. Another member of the crew had been chief officer aboard a ship on the Hamburg-American Line before the war. He had married his wife in New York and even had a brother in the U.S. Navy.

Once the *U-156* cleared the North Sea, Feldt positioned the nose of his submarine southwest and cautiously advanced toward the western Atlantic. His orders were clear: sink enemy ships and sink them often. On June 26, Feldt turned his guns on the British steamer *Tortuguero*, two hundred miles northwest of Ireland. Feldt seemed more concerned with sinking ships than saving sailors, and twelve crew members on the steamer followed their ship to the bottom of the sea. While the sinking of merchant ships was appreciated back in Berlin, the Kaiserliche Marine undoubtedly wanted the *U-156* to sink them closer to the United States and, in turn, cause unrest among coastal populations. More specifically, once Feldt reached the North American coast, he was instructed to mine and patrol approaches to American and Canadian ports. In addition, if a situation presented itself, the crew of the *U-156* was directed to capture an American or Canadian vessel and outfit it as an enemy raider, which would undoubtedly cause consternation amongst the Allies. Therefore, after engaging the steamer, the *U-156* left the eastern Atlantic and made a beeline for the American coast.

In London, Admiral William S. Sims, the United States' attaché to the Royal Navy, understood that the eastern seaboard had to be the raider's destination. "There was every expectation that Germany would send submarines to the western Atlantic, where they could prey upon our shipping and could possibly bombard our ports," Sims had projected earlier in the war.

On June 29, three days after the *U-156* sank the *Tortuguero*, Sims sent a cable to his counterparts in Washington suggesting that the *U-156* was likely heading west but lamented, "Her field of operation [is] not yet known." Sims even went so far as to suggest where and when the raider might bob out of the sea. The submarine, according to the prophetic Sims, "cannot reach longitude of Nantucket before July 15. Shall keep Department informed."

\*\*\*

Earlier that month, another German super submarine, the *U-151*, made a mockery of the U.S. Navy when it sank seven merchant schooners off the American coast in one day—it was one of the greatest single-day achievements of any U-boat during the entire war. In the days that followed, the raider continued to sink additional ships, her rampage leaving 450 men adrift at sea. In the coming days, these lifeboats would wash ashore all across the mid-Atlantic, causing mass panic up and down the East Coast.

The *New York Evening Post* sighed, "Well, they are here at last." The *Philadelphia Public Ledger* was more grim: "The waters within less than a hundred miles of the New Jersey coast are as full of peril as the waters of the North Sea or the English Channel." "Where was the powerful American scout and destroyer fleet?" one newspaper editor bemoaned. The jab was subtle, but it was clear that the press was not impressed with the U.S. Navy.

Some papers fueled the hysteria with rumors, which, in turn, fueled additional rumors. U-boats were ready, willing and able, one report said, to launch "especially constructed incendiary bombs" at New York City. In New Jersey, there were stories that German spies had landed at Cape May and had sprayed "disease germs" along the state's shoreline.

Regardless of whether this scuttlebutt was true, some coastal ports were shuttered, New York City's skyline was darkened and, in a show of force, antiaircraft guns were mounted on the Palisades overlooking the Hudson River.

In Manhattan, American agents raided German clubs looking for men who reportedly had "exulted" in the recent U-boat successes offshore. Outside these clubs, the growing crowd cheered and jeered each time a German was dragged to the waiting patrol wagon. Some of the more aggressive anti-German bystanders had to be restrained.

The hysteria was not confined to the mid-Atlantic; panic over the submarine scare spread hundreds of miles up the East Coast. In New England, mysterious light signals were reported, and it was decided by some to darken coastal towns and cover windows that faced the sea. Henry James, a teenager living on Cape Cod, noted how "a bed sheet, hung from a second-story window to air, was ordered removed by armed guards who suspected it might be a signal of some importance." In Boston, the lights that illuminated the bright gold dome of the Massachusetts State House were dimmed in an effort to not attract unnecessary attention from enemy submarines that might be lurking offshore.

Foreigners, such as a German artist who was casually painting in the vicinity of the Naval Radio Station in North Truro on Cape Cod, were arrested. Other "aliens" were taken into custody after authorities learned they had maps of the shoreline. In some coastal areas, foreigners simply were not allowed, while in others, identification cards became mandatory for sailors entering and exiting. U.S. senator Benjamin Tillman of South Carolina boasted that America would "hunt down these damned devils and wipe them off the face of the Earth." For the next week, the navy canvassed the eastern seaboard in search of the menacing U-boat. However, despite the vast dragnet, the submarine escaped.

"This is a warning of what later wars may bring," the boarding officer of the *U-151* cautioned after he returned to port in Germany. "For the day will come when submarines will think no more of a voyage across the Atlantic than they do now of a raid across the North Sea…America's isolation is now a thing of the past."

***

While her sister ship, the *U-151*, sailed east back to Germany, the *U-156* remained undetected and continued her cruise west toward the mid-Atlantic. Captain Feldt and his crew sank additional Allied and neutral ships as they sailed, and they began to sow the sea south of Long Island with mines. The raider did this under a cloak of secrecy, concealed from American forces for nine whole days. Now that the raider was so close to the coast and U.S. shipping lanes, she could do far more damage by laying mines than trying to wage battle with torpedoes and shells. It was a change of tactics; instead of stalking her prey, like a cat would a mouse, she laid countless traps. The "cat" would then retreat from the scene, hide in the shadows and let the "mousetraps" do the work for her. With

USS *San Diego*. *Library of Congress*.

the deck gun, Feldt could control the destiny of the submarine's targets and fire a warning shot to alert the crew. However, the mine was a more vicious weapon. Partly hidden beneath the surface, mines were hard to detect and typically exploded against a ship without warning. The fate of the vessel depended on where the mine struck, and the lives of the crew members rested on their ability to think quickly.

On the morning of July 19, the armored cruiser USS *San Diego* was en route from Portsmouth, New Hampshire, to New York City. Once there, she was to join a convoy of ships and begin the often-perilous transatlantic trek to France, escorting troops and supplies to the western front.

Below deck, lucky sailors—those who had been given liberty once they arrived in the Big Apple—were hastily sewing buttons and scrubbing grease stains from their uniforms. Others were lathering their faces for one last shave. If the sailors were lucky, they might find companionship when they hit shore.

Submarines were on the minds of everyone on the ship. Captain Harley Christy had ordered the *San Diego* to zigzag at a speed of fifteen knots in an effort to steer "a safe and proper course [and] minimize the dangers from submarines and mines." Despite all the precautions taken by Christy and his crew, at 11:05 a.m., an explosion ripped through the hull on the port side of the ship, instantly killing three American sailors. The blast was seen and heard in places as far away as Point of Woods, Long Island—a distance of ten miles—where hotel guests were enjoying a warm summer morning on the beach.

Captain Christy assumed the ship had been torpedoed and sounded the "submarine defense" alert. Gun crews rushed to their stations. If the ship had been torpedoed, the U-boat's wake or periscope would hopefully be visible off the portside. Christy's ordered his sailors to "fire at anything that looks like a submarine," and for the next ten minutes, according to one sailor, crew members "fired at most any object that met their eyes." The captain also instructed the bridge to "full speed ahead," an order that was obeyed until rushing salt water silenced the ship's engines.

Unsure of the totality of the damage, the captain withheld the order to abandon ship but reached for the radio to send an SOS. Unfortunately, the explosion had rendered the radio useless. Christy then turned to one of his trusted officers, a Lieutenant Bright, and asked him to assemble a team and make fast in one of the ship's lifeboats for Fire Island. Once on shore, the officer was to rouse every possible ship he could find and send them in the direction of the sinking cruiser.

As the minutes ticked by, the ship began to list more and more to her port side. Although the *San Diego* was clearly sinking, the sailors were ordered to remain at their posts. Hoping to maintain command among the chaos, one officer reportedly declared, "If anyone jumps before [the order of] abandon ship is given, I'll shoot him."

The cruiser continued to list to the port, and soon water was lapping up against the deck. By now, the captain knew the *San Diego* would sink, so he finally ordered the crew to abandon ship. Christy then turned to his gunnery officer and said, "Keep firing. Keep firing as long as you can serve the guns." Gun crews on the port side of the ship remained at their stations until the ocean rushed into the guns' barrels.

Then the *San Diego*'s smokestacks broke free, one of which crashed down on an unsuspecting sailor, killing him. Sailors frantically began launching lifeboats, but unfortunately, some on the port side were smashed to pieces when they hit the water. All eyes instead turned to the remaining rafts on the ship's starboard side. Sailors carefully began to unhook the lifeboats and lower them into the sea, but regrettably, another sailor was killed in the mêlée when one of these lifeboats fell on his head.

One sailor took matters into his own hands. Just as the ship began to submerge below the surface, he took a knife and slashed loose a pile of lumber that had been stowed safely on deck. The wood rolled off the deck and into the sea. The sailor followed and, with the help of his fellow seamen, began to fashion a life raft.

With the ship almost entirely under water, sailors desperately splashed about the oily sea and swam toward the nearest lifeboat. Others were left clinging to whatever flotsam they could find. With arms and legs kicking wildly in the ocean, it was impossible to account for every member of the crew, but one of the more prominent members of the ship was missing.

Inside the doomed ship, Captain Christy realized he was running out of time. From the bridge, he lumbered down two separate ladders before making a series of awkward jumps and landing on the deck. As the cruiser slowly capsized, a sailor shouted, "There's the skipper! I can see his bald head." Loud cheers erupted around the sinking ship. Christy ran along the hull and onto the now exposed keel, pausing for a moment as if to bid adieu, and then jumped eight feet into the water below. The captain was the last man to leave the ship alive. One sailor, still stuck in the crow's nest, was not as fortunate and drowned when the ship finally pitched.

The last of the smokestacks finally broke free and slapped the ocean like rifle shots. Then the cruiser bobbed upside down for about a minute or two before it vanished beneath the surface in sea of bubbles. Perhaps as many as one hundred men were sucked down with the ship, but all managed to swim safely back to the surface.

It had taken only twenty-eight minutes for the *San Diego* to sink.

The disciplined sailors—some safe in lifeboats, some treading water at sea—kept up their spirits by singing patriotic tunes. The captain, now safe in a boat, hoisted the Stars and Stripes for all to see, and the sailors just about lost it. Hooting and hollering, the cold, wet seamen cheered their captain and broke into the "Star-Spangled Banner."

\*\*\*

At 1:20 p.m., more than two hours after the *San Diego* struck the mine, Lieutenant Bright and his team finally reached the beach in their lifeboat. Hastily assembled for the mission, some of Bright's crew were partly clothed; one seaman was wearing what resembled a sack. Another sailor had only half of his face shaved. On shore, Bright and his cohorts rallied the local populace, and soon crafts of all shapes and sizes were steaming fast toward the location where the *San Diego* was last seen. Unbeknownst to Bright and the crowd assembled on the beach, a pilot had seen the ship sinking and was already assembling a convoy of ships and planes from the coast guard and navy.

En route to assist in the rescue, one ship happened upon an ominous sight—fins! "My vessel passed a school of perhaps twenty sharks, which were feeding on the body of a small whale," recalled the captain. "The sight gave me a scare, for I was afraid they were also after the men in the water." Fortunately, the sharks were kept at bay, and the majority of the *San Diego*'s nearly 1,200-member crew was rescued by 3:00 p.m., although it would take days to account for every individual seaman aboard the ship.

Converging from air and sea alike, ships and airplanes worked in concert with one another to locate and destroy the *U-156* that afternoon and into the next morning.

"We had our first real excitement at the air station," recalled a pilot with the First Yale Unit based in Long Island. "We sent out every plane that could be made to fly." At one point, the posse cornered what they assumed was the enemy raider. Trigger-happy airplanes dive-bombed the gurgling bubbles rising from the sea. "Several of the fellows," said the pilot, "went so far as to claim credit for having sunk the submarine."

Then, remembered a sailor on scene, "a flood of wreckage began to float to the surface—including papers and photos identifying the supposed submarine."

According to the pilot, "What really happened was that the bombs dropped by the planes brought up great quantities of air and wreckage from the *San Diego* itself."

The *U-156* had disappeared.

Captain Feldt and his crew had raised the stakes and brought the war just ten miles off the American coast. The loss of the *San Diego* was a severe blow to the U.S. Navy; the ship was considered one of best-armored cruisers in the fleet. It was also the only American warship lost in the western Atlantic during the entire war. In London, Admiral Sims went as far as saying that the loss of the *San Diego* was the "only real victory" of the German submarine raids on America.

In the immediate aftermath, there was considerable debate as to what, exactly, had sunk the *San Diego*. If it were a torpedo, as some had suggested, the raider might still be lurking nearby. However, if a mine had caused the explosion, the enemy submarine would likely be long gone. Unbeknownst to the U.S. Navy, the *U-156* was nowhere near Long Island on the morning of July 20. Somewhere, far to the east, Captain Feldt and his crew gleefully listened to reports of the *San Diego*'s sinking on their radio.

The super submarine had escaped. Where the raider would surface next was anyone's guess.

The cruise of the *U-156*. *Chuck Kacsur*.

\*\*\*

On the "elbow" of Cape Cod, in Orleans, Massachusetts, Helen Higgins was in town visiting her aunt Lottie. The weather outside was stifling. In an effort to avoid the oppressive conditions, the two women took to the front piazza, which overlooked beautiful Nauset Harbor. The porch offered shade, and if the weather cooperated, the sea might yield a breeze. For the past couple days, the two women allegedly had been watching a submarine bobbing about offshore. "It would surface every now and then," recalled Ms. Higgins. "We thought it was charging its batteries [and] naturally, we thought it was one of ours…"

## CHAPTER 4
# THE GERMANS ARE COMING

*We're absolutely safe here, so close to shore.*
—*Captain Joseph Perry*

July 21, 1918, once again dawned hot and hazy in Orleans, Massachusetts. A heat wave had been choking the state for days; several Bay Staters had already perished because of the extreme temperatures, so residents and vacationers alike had flocked to the cooler coast with the goal of escaping the oppressive inland conditions. If there were any chance of a breeze, those in Orleans would feel it.

Boston is almost ninety miles from Orleans, and the Sunday papers, brought in by train, would not arrive until noon. That morning, members of the local gentry passed the time on their respective porches thumbing through the pages of Saturday's periodicals instead. Inside, Cape Codders read about the sinking of the USS *San Diego* off Fire Island, New York, by a U-boat, one of two super submarines rumored to be operating along the coast. Reports differed as to what actually sank the American warship (a torpedo or a mine) and how many lives had been lost; one of the two muster rolls went down with the ship, and sixty-two souls were missing and feared drowned. The war was indeed coming closer to home. Having leafed through every page at least twice, cottagers now used their papers to fan their sweaty faces and necks.

By mid-morning, the sun was already blazing; thankfully, a layer of fog was keeping the rays at bay. Everyone knew the weather would only get worse as morning gave way to afternoon. Some residents were even debating whether to go to church—it was simply too hot. Many decided to wait out the heat by sitting on their front porches and staring out toward the sea. Visibility was less than two miles, and the ocean was smooth—so smooth, one resident noted, that "you could have landed a canoe on a beach without any problem at all."

It was undoubtedly a peaceful Sunday morning.

***

Offshore, the 120-foot steel tugboat *Perth Amboy* chugged south along the outer arm of the Cape en route to the Virginia Capes. The sea was quiet, absent of swells, and the Atlantic softly slapped against the ship's side. The five-year-old tug had four barges in tow: the *Lansford, Barge 766, Barge 703* and *Barge 740*. Only the *766* contained any cargo—stone, or more specifically, Cape Ann granite. Two of the other barges were filled with ballast, and the fourth was empty. Overall, it was a light load for the tug *Perth Amboy*.

The five vessels carried a total of thirty-two people; many were Portuguese from the town of New Bedford who had recently left the Old World for a better life in America. Also included were four women (wives of the four barge captains) and five children. It was customary for the captains' families to accompany them aboard their barges.

Shortly after 8:00 a.m., the *Perth Amboy* and her quarry rounded Highland Light, located on the "fist" of Cape Cod in Provincetown, and then steamed

The tugboat *Perth Amboy. From the collection of William P. Quinn.*

Nauset Beach Light Station. *Courtesy of Jeremy D'Entremont.*

south toward the "elbow." James P. Tapley, the captain of the tug, yawned, checked his watch and then proceeded to his cabin to rest his eyes. His sleep had been interrupted earlier that morning when the tug had pulled into Gloucester, Massachusetts, to collect one of the four barges in his tow.

In addition, before daybreak, one of Captain Tapley's crew members woke the captain a second time to report what he thought was a periscope protruding out of the ocean off the port side of the tug. Captain Tapley immediately dismissed the idea, noting that German U-boats would not wander so close to shore because the coast was constantly being patrolled by sub-chasers.

Despite reports trickling in about the *San Diego*, crew members believed they were safe in the shallow waters just off the coast. Captain Joseph Perry, who operated the last barge in tow, was sitting on deck, half-dressed and taking in the morning sun. While reading a newspaper, the nonchalant Perry glanced at the sunbathers visible on Nauset Beach to the west and, echoing Captain Tapley, assured his worried wife, who was cooking in the kitchen below, "We're absolutely safe here, so close to the shore."

Others making the journey were probably more concerned with the area's notorious sandbars and storms; three thousand shipwrecks had occurred here over the course of the past three hundred years. Nevertheless, the sailors aboard the tug and barges were also confident. The *Perth Amboy* "was the finest tug in the fleet," boasted the manager of the freight company, and although the Cape was notorious for nasty weather, on July 21, 1918, the sea was eerily calm.

At 10:15 a.m., the tug and barges passed Nauset Beach Light Station* in Eastham. The twenty-five-foot structure sat on a bluff some sixty feet above the sea. Three quick flashes of flame from the tower's kerosene lantern reminded the tugboat crew that she was on course, safe away from the shore.

Later, once the tug and its barges rounded the Cape's "elbow," they would start steaming west. The construction of the Cape Cod Canal in 1914 had greatly reduced the travel time from Boston to New York, but Lehigh's management was not interested in paying the exorbitant toll. Instead, like countless ships that had made this same journey before her, the *Perth Amboy* and her barges would stick to the outer arm and avoid the fee.

***

On shore, Number One Surfman William Moore was on watch in the tower at U.S. Coast Guard Station Number 40, in Orleans, about four miles west-southwest from the *Perth Amboy* and her barges. Moore scanned the horizon, constantly looking for ships in peril, but with the ocean so tranquil, it seemed highly unlikely that he and his cohorts would have any missions that day. Traffic out at sea had been slow thus far; only two ships had steamed past his lookout. One was the *Arlington*, and the other was the *J.B. King*, both colliers transporting coal.

While Moore maintained watch, Captain Robert F. Pierce, the station's keeper, and the five other surfmen at the station that morning did their best to pass the time in their quarters below the tower. Some sipped coffee, while others stretched their legs atop their cots. Later in the day, the surfmen might drill, but for the time being, they were content to put their feet up and enjoy the quiet morning.

Moore yawned and continued to squint into the haze. Coming into view in the northeast was what appeared to be a large tugboat towing a number of barges—nothing out of the ordinary. They were puttering slowly along the Cape's arm, smoke belching from the tug's stack. Moore yawned again and then wiped his sweaty brow. The warm weather enhanced the lackadaisical atmosphere—conditions that underscored it was Sunday.

***

---

* Nauset Light is the lighthouse that Cape Cod Potato Chips uses on its bags.

View looking northeast from Station Number 40. *From* Life Savers of Cape Cod.

Two miles from the *Perth Amboy* and her quarry, the seining ship *Rose*, captained by Marsi Schuill, was on its way to join up with a fleet of schooners from Gloucester fishing for mackerel thirty-five miles out at sea. Captain Schuill was late, but he was determined to get to the school before the mackerel had dispersed. Suddenly, through the mid-morning haze, Captain Schuill saw what resembled a giant whale breaching the surface. Having heard rumors of U-boats prowling offshore, the captain shouted below deck and ordered his engineman to "full speed ahead" toward shore.

"We…were startled to see a submarine break water…with the water sparkling in the sunlight as it rolled off her sides," recalled Schuill. The mackerel would have to wait. "We didn't stop to go fishing—we got into the first fog we ever appreciated."

\*\*\*

Ignoring the *Rose*, the *U-156* crept out of the fog and inched closer toward the unsuspecting *Perth Amboy* and her barges, floating helplessly to the west of the sub. Captain Richard Feldt's string of successful victories had put the U.S. Navy on edge, but so far, his raider had eluded detection despite a tightening dragnet. For reasons that largely remain speculative, Feldt determined that the tug and barges that appeared in his periscope were opportune targets, so he gave the order to open fire.

***

Just before ten thirty that morning,[*] a deckhand on the *Perth Amboy* was startled by the sight of something white skipping through the water. The mysterious object passed wide of the tug, to the stern. Stunned and confused, the deckhand said nothing.[†]

***

At that same moment, back on shore, Giuseppi Massetti, a fisherman who had just returned to port, was staring out toward the sea. All of a sudden, he noticed "a spurt of flame, a puff of smoke, then sort of a shrieking, whining noise."

In the bluffs above the fisherman, Dr. Joshua Danforth Taylor, a well-to-do physician vacationing from east Boston, observed something offshore that did not fit the seascape: "I saw the boat and almost at the same time heard the first crash of its guns."

A great thunderous roar ripped through the quiet summer morning in Orleans. Those along the bluff and near the beach were confused—no one was expecting rain.

Suddenly, an object crashed into the beach below the doctor's cottage, sending sand high into the air in every direction.

Down on the beach, Massetti described the place of impact "as though a steam shovel had gouged out a cellar."

Neither knew it at the time, but the fisherman and the physician had just witnessed a historical event: the German projectile that landed on the beach was the first enemy fire to strike the American mainland since the War of 1812. Though the United States had fought border wars with Mexico in the 1840s (and more blood had been spilled during the American Civil War than in all other U.S. military conflicts combined), this strange raid on the normally peaceful arm of Cape Cod was the first time the American continent had been attacked by a foreign foe in over one hundred years.

In the distance, a church bell began to ring. It was 10:30 a.m.

---

[*] Reports of the time the attack started differ slightly. Most accounts suggest the *Perth Amboy* was attacked at 10:30 a.m., but others suggest she was attacked as early as 10:15 a.m. By 10:30 a.m., many on shore were alerted to the commotion going on out at sea, which leads the author to believe that the first salvo fired by the U-boat occurred shortly before 10:30 a.m.
[†] Reports also differ as to whether the first projectiles fired by the submarine were torpedoes or shells. However, they were likely shells because torpedoes cost more money.

***

Back on the tug, the perplexed deckhand saw two more streaks cut through the sea, but they, too, steered wide of the ship. Some commotion had occurred behind him on shore, but things were happening too quickly for him to surmise what was going on. Finally, he came to his senses and cried out a warning, but it was too late; a shell from one of the sub's two 5.9-inch deck guns, shrieked through the sky and crashed into the tug's pilothouse, sending flames into the air.

The structure partially collapsed on top of John Bogovich, the helmsman who was steering the ship, knocking him unconscious. The shell, Bogovich recalled later, "Came right into the pilothouse and passed through it (then) made a big crash."

Bogovich, regaining consciousness, was scooped up off the deck by a fellow crew member. Stunned and shaken, he noticed that his right arm was nearly severed, with two deep, jagged wounds above his elbow. His left shoulder was also bleeding. It was not known whether his injuries were the result of the shell's shrapnel, the pilothouse that had collapsed on top of him or a combination of the two.

Fellow seaman John Zitz was also struck during the opening barrage: "I was sleeping in my bunk when 'Bang!'…I woke up and half the pilothouse was gone, the tug was afire, and part of my right hand was gone." Zitz's fingers were terribly bruised after being struck by flying splinters of wood and steel. The outside of his knee was also bleeding.

Like Zitz, Captain Tapley was fast asleep when the tug received its initial volley. At the sound of the first blast, thirty-nine-year-old Tapley staggered out on deck and knuckled the dreams from his eyes.

"My room adjoining the pilothouse was completely destroyed with everything in it," Tapley lamented. Coming into view, just off his port bow, loomed an enormous submarine.

"There was nothing in sight in any direction," said Tapley, "when suddenly, to the east of us, there seemed to rise out of the haze this massive hull which looked to us like a battleship." Half stunned, Tapley quipped, "This, I was sure, was the source of the trouble."

Tapley braced for impact, but few of the U-boat's shells hit their target, instead pounding the ocean around the *Perth Amboy* and sending fountains of water up in to the sky.

"I never saw a more glaring example of rotten marksmanship," said Captain Tapley. "Shots went wild repeatedly and but few that were fired scored hits."

The captain swallowed hard and wondered where the next round might land. He knew it was only a matter of time until the sub scored another hit, possibly a knockout.

"We were powerless against such an enemy," Tapley moaned. "All that we could do was to stand there and take what they sent us."

Zitz looked out in the direction of the U-boat, wishing he had a gun.

*\*\*\**

Reuben Hopkins, one of the surfmen at Station Number 40, left the lookout tower earlier in the morning "to catch forty winks" and was one of the lifesavers nestled comfortably on a cot inside the station. Like the keeper, Robert Pierce, Hopkins, too, was a native Cape Codder, having graduated from Orleans High School just five years earlier. Hopkins's father only had enough money saved up for one of his ten children to go to college, and that honor went to Reuben's younger brother George. So Reuben instead

Reuben Hopkins. *Courtesy of Stephen Hopkins.*

entered the U.S. Coast Guard. By 1918, the handsome twenty-two-year-old surfman found himself posted at Station Number 40.

Hopkins had a hunch that a U-boat attack might be imminent during the summer of 1918. He had heard reports that several ships had been torpedoed along the coast, and he noticed something peculiar in the way ships had been traveling past the surf station—most were grouped in convoys of four or five in an effort to protect themselves from enemy subs.

Suddenly a "hard thump" jolted Hopkins awake. Sensing something might be amiss, he jumped from his bed and scrambled to the watchtower to join Moore, who was excitedly pointing his finger seaward. As he peered into the mid-morning fog, Hopkins saw something he would never forget:

THE GERMANS ARE COMING

> [I] *observed…a tug and tow of four barges. A little further offshore, and perhaps a quarter-mile from the tug, I could discern a submarine lying low and broadside to the beach…She was difficult to see because of the haze. I had barely taken all this in when I saw the flash of a gun on the submarine. The shell landed in the water aft of the tug, which by now had come to a dead stop. The tug took a direct hit on the pilothouse.*

Moore climbed down the tower and informed the station's keeper, Robert Pierce, that there were "heavy guns firing on a tow of barges east, northeast from the station." Pierce, a seasoned seaman who had worked as a lifesaver for nearly thirty years, had never heard anything like this before in his life. He instinctively ordered the surfboat dragged out of the station, but as evidence of a submarine offshore became increasingly clear, the keeper began to contemplate what, exactly, he should do next.

***

Two miles to the north, curious townspeople who had heard the commotion going on offshore began to spill out of their homes and descend on Nauset Beach.

"The concussion of the shells lifted the fog," remembered Major Clifford Harris, the local commander of the Massachusetts State Guard, who lived above Nauset Beach. "I could see the flames coming up out of the forward hatch. In all, about twenty shots were fired at the tug."

Some of the shells from the sub were skipping across the water and soaring through the sky, causing fear and confusion among the residents of Orleans. "With the first shot, there was a rush of people to the beach," Harris recalled. "Two shots came up to the beach scattering the crowd. One shot struck on the shore also at Nauset Harbor."

One shell allegedly zipped over the head of a man who was shingling the roof of his cottage, while another reportedly landed a mile inland near the home of a Mrs. Weston Taylor, who was working in her kitchen at the time. "It was as if a gigantic rocket came over the house," Mrs. Taylor recalled. "There was a great hissing and sizzling sounds. It did not seem to be more than a few feet above the roof."

Mrs. Taylor rushed outside to see where the object would land and turned her attention to nearby Meeting House Pond. Evelyn Ham and several other young women were in that pond escaping the heat. They watched as the shell splashed a few hundred yards away. Either ignorant or brave, they were not particularly frightened and continued to frolic about as if nothing had happened.

Only a handful of witnesses were fortuitous enough to see the historic shells crashing onto the shore, but countless others heard the roar from the super submarine's dual deck guns, and all agreed that the bombardment was extremely loud. To someone on the island of Nantucket, some thirty miles away, the sub's guns sounded like "low, rolling thunder." But in Orleans, the barrage was far more immediate. One resident claimed the shelling "shook the earth."

Another witness described the sound of the bombardment as that of a "freight train going through a tunnel."

Richard Bonnell said the shells sounded like a "thump...like an explosion, like an earthquake."

Howard Chase remembered his house shaking and the dishes rattling.

Herbert Gibbs simply thought someone had fallen down upstairs. After three or four repetitions of the sound, at short intervals, he knew something else was happening, and his family began to wander in the direction of the reports.

Ten-year-old Lou DeLano and his father were walking downtown to the livery stables to pick up the Sunday papers, an enjoyable weekly ritual for the young man. At first, they attributed the blasts they heard offshore to the U.S. military. However, today was a Sunday—and a Sunday morning, to boot. The navy would never commence a barrage this early on a Sunday, would it?

Amos Lefavour and his family were some of the few who had braved the sweltering conditions that morning to go to church. Like many, Lefavour described the sound coming from the sea as that of thunder. "No one thought anymore of church," Lefavour recalled. He and other worshippers left their pews and started toward the beach. "All seemed to think that the dreaded, expected...bombardment of the Cape had started." Defiant, and perhaps with too much bravado, Lefavour then boasted, "Cape Cod has met the German submarine menace and is not afraid."

Whether or not the townsfolk of Orleans were actually equipped to repel an invasion was debatable, but one thing was certain: Orleans, Massachusetts, was under attack. Ever vulnerable to nor'easters and gales, the "elbow" of Cape Cod was now facing a new peril: the German navy, which was now on America's doorstep. Tales of U-boats prowling the Atlantic were indeed disconcerting, but to Americans, and specifically to those vacationing on sleepy Cape Cod, the war seemed like a European affair, whose outcome would be decided in the muddy trenches on the western front, not on the sandy beaches of Cape Cod. Some in Orleans expected the worst and assumed the attack to be the beginning of a massive East Coast invasion.

Soon, cottagers feared, the beastly German Hun might storm the Cape's beaches and rape its villages.

Upon hearing the sound of the first few reports, one prophetic woman jumped out of her chair and shouted, "The Germans! The Germans!"

Another frightened citizen rang the office of the deputy sheriff and shouted, "The Germans are coming after us! Hurry up and come down here and save Orleans!"

Major Clifford Harris was not taking any chances. A veteran of the Spanish-American War, Harris was known to everyone in town as *Major* Harris, never *Mr.* Harris. On that frightful morning, the major feared the worst, and shortly after the first few shots were fired, he rushed to the phone and mustered his troops. If Germans were going to splash ashore here in Orleans like the British had done one hundred years earlier, the major and his local militia would be ready.

## CHAPTER 5

# YOU DON'T HAVE TO COME BACK

*From a quiet Sunday morning, everything in a minute or two was confusion.*
*—Captain Charles Ainsleigh*

A board the *Perth Amboy*, the injured sailors, Bogovich and Zitz, writhed anxiously about on deck, not knowing where the next round from the submarine's guns would land.

"The fire was very erratic, and the gunners seemed to be nervous," Captain Tapley construed. As many as twenty shots were fired at the tug—"enough shots to sink the entire Lehigh Valley fleet," Tapley believed—but the steel ship refused to sink.

Still, the pockmarked *Perth Amboy* was essentially crippled. Flames licked what remained of the pilothouse, and the crew members, who were huddled helplessly in the tug's stern, decided to abandon ship. Around that time, Captain Tapley finally noticed that his helmsman was injured; through Bogovitch's arm was "a hole about the size of a half silver dollar." The helmsman was bleeding profusely. Some of his fellow sailors feared he would lose part of his arm, while others thought he might die. With his one good hand, Zitz hastily unpacked life preservers while other sailors helped Bogovich board the tug's lifeboat, which took, as Tapley recalled, just four minutes. The captain then hoisted a white flag, signaling a truce of sorts, and together the sixteen refugees from the tug started rowing toward the beach some two to three miles away. All the while, shells from the sub continued to fall indiscriminately into the sea around the frightened sailors.

The *Perth Amboy*'s lifeboat rows to shore. *Courtesy of the Orleans Historical Society*.

The *U-156*, content with the outcome of this one-sided chess match, pivoted away from the disabled tug and inched closer toward the *Lansford*, the first of the four barges trailing the *Perth Amboy*.

Aboard the *Lansford*, Captain Charles Ainsleigh; his wife, Marguerite; and their two sons, Charles and Jack, had been enjoying a quiet Sunday morning. Also aboard the barge was the family dog, Rex, as well a handful of egg-laying hens, which had been nervously clucking away since the shelling began.

"I was mixing bread when the shooting started," Marguerite said. "Suddenly I heard my husband cry, 'Come quick, Mother!' and I ran up on deck and saw the water bubbling all around us." Shells from the *U-156*'s guns began to pepper the water in front of their barge.

"From a quiet Sunday morning, everything in a minute or two was confusion," said Captain Ainsleigh.

Ainsleigh's eldest son, Charles, recalled how the guns "made more noise than any guns I ever heard."

"She opened up with a rain of shells upon us, but few of them struck the barges," said Ainsleigh. Echoing Captain Tapley, he added, "Such poor marksmanship I never saw. Whether they were just playing with us, it is hard to tell."

Marguerite was more direct—she called the German gunners "cowards" and added, "we couldn't see the submarine then because of a light fog bank that hung low over the water. Then as the fog lifted we saw the U-boat and three fast flashes of flame."

Joseph Perry, the captain of *Barge 740*, who had earlier assured his wife that submarines in these waters were rare, also witnessed the poor aim of the German gunners as they repeatedly missed the *Lansford*. Eventually, however, the raider lined its sights correctly, and volleys began to strike the Ainsleighs' barge.

Perry recalled, "I saw a black object about five feet from the barge *Lansford*, [and] as I looked, the black object exploded."

"One after another," remembered Captain Ainsleigh, "the shells got to us until there were five or six holes in our barge. One of the German shells had exploded amidship, blowing off the deck hatches from within...[and] before I could say 'Jack Robinson'* another shell ripped up the planking at my feet."

"There was a terrible explosion," remembered Marguerite. "My husband pitched forward crying, 'They got us Mother...keep down!'"

In the mêlée, Captain Ainsleigh was wounded in both arms by flying debris.

"There was a blinding flash and I was half stunned. Blood was streaming from my hands and arms. The flag was torn from my grasp. She settled at the bow with the stern out of the water."

Still stunned from the explosion, Captain Ainsleigh collected himself just in time to see the "hull of the dripping submarine" emerge from the haze. With the U-boat closing in fast, Marguerite tore up a bedsheet and bandaged her husband up as best she could. Then Ainsleigh and his family decided to abandon ship. The *Lansford*—their barge, their *home*—was now sinking. Soon all they owned would sit on the floor of the Atlantic.

*** 

For the past several minutes, Captain Marsi Schuill and the crew of the mackerel schooner *Rose* had been watching the entire attack from a distance.

"I see that sub, looking like a big tin whale spouting hellfire," recalled Schuill. "[Then] the deck guns swing around towards us and there was a flash, and a shell came slipping along the water..."

Fearing they might be the raider's next target, Schuill's crew "started in full speed for shore." During her dash to the coast, the fleeing seiner was sprayed by the submarine's machine gun.

"Several shots came within 10 feet of us," remembered Schuill. "All hands thought their time had come."

Luckily, the *Rose* escaped unscathed. Once Captain Schuill's ship was closer to shore and out of range, the crew dropped anchor and started toward the beach in their dory.

---

* To say that something was "as fast as Jack Robinson" implied that it happened very quickly.

Unfortunately for the mariners aboard the remaining three barges, there were still plenty of targets left for Captain Feldt and the crew of the *U-156*.

\*\*\*

Back on shore, at U.S. Coast Guard Station Number 40, Captain Robert Pierce and his band of six surfmen, including William Moore and Reuben Hopkins, were the first line of defense against the raider from the deep. But they had little in their surf station to combat the arsenal of a German U-boat, whose aim, as Hopkins argued, was "damned good." In fact, the lifesavers carried no weapons at all. On the wall was a list of instructions to follow in the event that an enemy vessel ever appeared offshore. "That was quite ridiculous to our minds," Hopkins noted. Few at the station ever imagined a submarine attack.

Rubbing his balding head with his hand, Pierce contemplated his options. Should the lifesavers launch their surfboat to rescue the sailors under enemy fire?

"It looked rather hard to be sent miles offshore in a small surfboat to a German submarine firing heavy guns," Pierce thought. It might very well be a death sentence, but the alternative was to sit on the sidelines and do nothing. Pierce knew his lifesavers might be the sailors' only hope.

The keeper picked up the telephone and dialed his superior officer, Superintendent George W. Bowley, stationed in Provincetown. Although he was younger than Pierce, Bowley came from a family of lifesavers, and like Pierce, he had been around boats and the ocean his entire life. Still, their combined experience did little to prepare them for something like this.

Captain Robert Pierce (left) of Station Number 40. *National Park Service.*

As they conferred, Pierce could see shells landing pell-mell three miles from his station. Precious moments ticked by, but eventually Bowley told Pierce to "launch a surfboat and rescue the people from the tow boat and the sinking barges." Pierce swallowed hard, walked outside and ordered his men to launch the surfboat.

Then, at 10:40 a.m., approximately ten minutes after the shelling commenced, Pierce used the station's phone to call the Chatham Naval Air Station, located seven miles to the south. If Pierce and his surfmen were going into the lion's den, they were going to need some help. The air station's new flying boats were equipped with bombs that packed a much bigger punch than anything the lifesavers had in their small surf station. Regrettably, it would take operators nearly ten minutes to transmit the urgent message to the air station so Pierce's message was simple and to the point: "Submarine sighted. Tug and three* barges being fired on, and one is sinking three miles off Coast Guard Station 40."

Pierce slammed the phone back on the receiver and then rushed to join Moore and the other lifesavers, who were in the process of launching the lifeboat. Before doing so, the keeper directed Reuben Hopkins, who was competent at signaling, to man the watchtower.

Pierce boarded last, from astern, giving the boat one last heave off the beach. On most rescue missions, waves would pummel the shore as lifesavers launched their craft, but that day the ocean was absent of surf. With a long oar, Pierce guided the craft in the direction of the submarine's shells. As the surfmen rowed headlong into the commotion, Pierce recalled the lifesaver's creed: "You have to go, but you don't have to come back."

\*\*\*

Captain Phillip B. Eaton was already flying high in the sky when the *U-156* commenced its attack on Orleans. The commander of the Chatham Naval Air Station had been out for hours searching for a lost dirigible that had gone missing two days earlier. In his absence, Lieutenant (JG) Elijah E. Williams, a North Carolinian with a southern drawl, was in command. Though he was ten miles from the commotion off Nauset Beach, the lieutenant was able to clearly identify the sound coming from the sea as shellfire.

"When I heard the firing I didn't wait for any [phone] message," Williams boasted. Instead, the proactive officer rushed toward the station's hangar in an effort to rouse the first pilot he could find.

---

* There were, in fact, *four* barges, not three. In their haste, the surfmen must have counted incorrectly.

Unfortunately, the station had two big problems: (1) the majority of Chatham's pilots, including Captain Eaton, had already been launched to search for a missing blimp, and (2) many of the pilots who remained on base were rumored to be off playing baseball against the crew of a minesweeper in Provincetown.

It was a Sunday morning, after all.

\*\*\*

Meanwhile, in Orleans, crowds of the curious continued to emerge from their summer homes and trekked toward Nauset Beach.

Shortly before 11:00 a.m., Dr. Taylor, the physician who saw the U-boat's first shell crash into the dunes below his summer cottage, telephoned his favorite newspaper, the *Boston Globe*.

"Hello! Is this the *Globe*?" Taylor inquired. "This is Dr. Taylor of East Boston. I am at Nauset on Cape Cod. There is a submarine battle going on offshore." The newsman on the other end of the line either rolled his eyes in disbelief or scrambled to find a typewriter. Perhaps he did both.

Peering out toward the sea, Taylor began to relay the scene: "There is a big German U-boat firing at a towboat and four barges, but you should see that firing—it is the worst ever. The fight is only a short distance from the shore and is plainly visible to all the cottagers here."

On and off for the next sixty minutes, Dr. Taylor provided live reports and commentary to the *Globe*. The newspaper later described Taylor's account as so graphic that it was as if the "men in the *Globe* office were also witnessing the unusual drama being played out on the oily waters off Orleans."

Taylor told the paper:

> *At first we thought the Hun was going to shell the houses along the beach, and a number of my neighbors came here to my place to take shelter because I have a good cellar. When it became apparent that the shots landing near us were simply poor attempts to hit the towboat and the four barges, people came out more freely, and the bolder ones are now seated on their cottage piazzas watching the fight…everybody here with an American flag has it flying from their houses.*

It was a gesture that, some witnesses claimed, attracted fire from the raider offshore.

\*\*\*

At 10:49 a.m., Lieutenant Williams finally managed to secure a Curtiss HS-1L flying boat—number 1693—and rallied a crew to fly it. One minute later, at 10:50 a.m., the Chatham Naval Air Station received the delayed alert from Robert Pierce at Station Number 40 confirming what Williams feared all along: a submarine attack!

"We got everybody to making these [flying] boats ready," said Williams. "All went along in orderly fashion as fast as we could go."

HS-1L number 1693 was one of the four planes that had been shipped to the air station just three weeks earlier, and on the morning of July 21, it was not yet ready for service. However, that hardly mattered since a submarine was shelling the mainland. In spite of its condition, the flying boat was quickly armed with a bomb and told to "shove off." Regrettably, a spark plug problem prohibited the plane from making any momentum down the water runway, and it was forced to return to the beach.

Seconds ticked by, but the executive officer acted quickly. Within minutes of initially receiving word of the attack, Lieutenant Williams secured a second flying boat—HS-1L number 1695.

However, this flying boat *also* had a problem: the plane's crankshaft had been giving pilots trouble, and it was in the process of being repaired. No one knew how long the plane would stay in the air. Despite this uncertainty, a twenty-seven-year-old ensign stepped forward and was determined to fly. His name was Eric Lingard.

The Harvard football star turned ice-making entrepreneur turned shipbuilder turned aviator would finally get his chance. Despite his thirst for bravado overseas, Lingard had been assigned stateside, and he thought he would never see any enemy action on this side

Ensign Eric Lingard. *Courtesy of the Middlesex School.*

of the Atlantic. Having grown up in Gloucester, Lingard was familiar with the Massachusetts coast, and as a pilot, he was obsessed with hitting his marks during target practice.

Needless to say, Ensign Eric Lingard was undoubtedly the right man for the job.

*** 

Positioned high atop Station Number 40's watchtower, Reuben Hopkins used his powerful binoculars to watch his cohorts close in on the *Perth Amboy*'s lifeboat, which was "loaded with her crew and a white flag showing was seen rounding her stern and pulling to the shore."

Hopkins's watch was briefly interrupted by a call from the Chatham Naval Air Station. Lieutenant Williams was having second thoughts. He wanted to determine whether the ship offshore was truly a German U-boat and not simply an American submarine. After all, false reports of enemy U-boats were commonplace in wartime America, especially during the summer of 1918. Hopkins, who needed no further evidence, was "hopping up and down

HS-1L flying boat takes to the sky. *Courtesy of the San Diego Air & Space Museum.*

with impatience." He thought the "times demanded action." Williams's slow southern drawl only added to Hopkins's frustration. The surfman composed himself and coolly told Williams, "It's highly unlikely an *American* submarine would be sinking *American* vessels."

"I'll see what I can do," Williams replied before hanging up the phone.

At 10:54 a.m., four minutes after Pierce's initial message reached the station, Lingard and his two-man crew took off from the water runway in Chatham and soared into the clouds. Flying through the mid-morning haze, Lingard aimed the nose of his plane north and then raced as fast as he could to Orleans. If things went as planned, his flying boat would reach Nauset Beach in just a few minutes.

*** 

By now, Pierce and his surfmen were within earshot of the *Perth Amboy*'s lifeboat, but they were also much closer to the *U-156*; the concussion from the U-boat's gunfire, in fact, blew the hats off two of the lifesavers. Worried that the surfmen might stray into the sub's shellfire, Captain Tapley shouted to Pierce from his lifeboat, "All have left the barges. My crew is here. For Christ's sake, don't go out where they are."

Captain Pierce recalled, "When about two-thirds of the way off to the sinking tug and four barges, we met the boat from the *Perth Amboy* with all her crew which had escaped."

Number One Surfman Bill Moore jumped aboard the *Perth Amboy*'s lifeboat and began to administer first aid to the wounded sailors, starting with John Bogovich, who by then was a semiconscious, bloody heap in the stern of the boat. Moore dug through his first aid kit and then wrapped a tourniquet above Bogovich's shattered arm to curtail the bleeding. It was quick work, but it seemed to do the trick. Moore then moved on to dress the wounds of John Zitz. Once his triage was complete, the surfman turned his eyes to the beach, and together with the survivors of the tug, he began to row furiously for shore.

Looking up at the sky, many wondered when help would arrive.

# CHAPTER 6

# THE COUNTERATTACK

*Gee, they are rotten shots.*
*—Jack Ainsleigh*

Flying north along Cape Cod's coast, Eric Lingard and his two-man crew were closing in on Nauset Beach.

Ensign Edward Shields sat alongside Lingard just forward of the plane's overhead power plant. Despite their proximity to each other, the

HS-1L flying boat high in the sky. *Courtesy of the San Diego Air & Space Museum.*

*Above*: Edward M. Shields, Lingard's assistant pilot. *U.S. Navy*.

*Right*: Edward H. Howard, Lingard's observer. *U.S. Navy*.

roar of the Liberty engine made communication difficult, and they were forced to shout and gesture.

Like Lieutenant Williams back at the air station, Shields doubted whether the crew would, in fact, come face to face with an enemy U-boat. "When we set out, we did not believe it was a submarine; we had so many false reports," he recalled.

Chief Special Mechanic Edward Howard manned the bomber's seat at the bow of the plane, his eyes scanning the horizon in search of the raider. Howard was an everyman—part observer, part bomber and, in the early days of aviation, part troubleshooter. When Ensign Lingard got the bulk of his seaplane over the sub, Howard would release the plane's Mark IV bomb, which, if things went according to plan, would put a quick end to the nightmare going on in the ocean below. Howard would have only one chance, however, as Lingard's flying boat carried only one bomb.

With a length of fifty-five inches and a diameter of almost one foot, the Mark IV was an imposing sight. The bomb contained 120 pounds of TNT, which, if dropped within one hundred feet of its target, could destroy a submarine. In fact, the Mark IV bomb blast was so powerful that pilots were prohibited from flying less than one thousand feet above their target during a bombing run. The force of the explosion, it was said, could rip the fabric from the flying boat's wings and send the plane plummeting to earth.

Howard's hand readied; from the bow of the plane, he could see Nauset Beach coming into view.

***

On board the *Lansford*, the injured Captain Ainsleigh and his family had clustered together in the stern of the ship. Rex, the Ainsleighs' beloved dog, was in the cabin when the firing began but had disappeared during the confusion. Unfortunately, the family had no time to look for him before they decided to abandon ship.

"I told [my son] that he had better gather his things together and get ready to get into the [life]boat," said Captain Ainsleigh. Instead, ten-year-old Jack raced back to the cabin and grabbed a .22-caliber rifle, a birthday gift his father had given his elder brother; a box of cartridges; and an American flag. "I'm going to shoot some of those Germans if they do kill us all," Jack screamed to no one in particular.

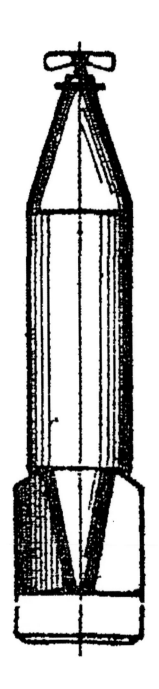

Mark IV bomb. *U.S. Army Corps of Engineers.*

Young Jack's fifteen minutes of fame had begun.

Aboard their lifeboat, the Ainsleigh family made sure to keep the barge between them and the sub and then "proceeded as swiftly as we could for Nauset Beach." En route to shore, young Jack tied his American flag to the end of a boathook and proudly waved it from the bow of the skiff for all to see.

Ainsleigh's elder son, Charles, waved something that packed a bigger punch—his .22-caliber rifle.

Jack Ainsleigh with his American flag and his brother's rifle. *From the collection of William P. Quinn.*

"I told him that his rifle could do nothing against the Germans—that the submarine's shell was too thick to be pierced by the tiny bullets—but he kept plotting away. If we had been equipped with a [better] gun I think we could have caused [the sub] much worry," boasted the proud father.

With the surfmen from Station Number 40 preoccupied rescuing the sailors from the *Perth Amboy*, local fishermen Clarence Robbin and Lawrence Hopkins met the Ainsleigh family near their sinking barge in a lobster skiff. The Ainsleighs were already secure in their own life raft, so the good Samaritans did the next best thing and attempted to pull aboard what personal belongings they could from the surf. It was largely a fruitless effort; many of their possessions were on their way to the ocean floor or drifting out to sea.

As the Ainsleighs approached the shore, the growing crowd that watching the spectacle from the beach saw Jack's Stars and Stripes and erupted into applause.

Once on shore, Jack told his admiring audience, "Gee, they are rotten shots."

"All were pretty cool," said one particular eyewitness on the beach, "but the youngster with the flag was the coolest of the lot."

Smiling, Dr. Taylor, who was still on the phone with the *Globe*, remarked, "[It's] great of the little chap…They will make a lot of him here as soon as the excitement has quieted down."

Captain Ainsleigh, too, felt a sense of satisfaction: "My little boy Jack appeared to enjoy the whole affair, and his display of courage is truly remarkable."

\*\*\*

Those on the beach then turned their attention toward the sky and saw a rickety flying boat appear on the southern horizon.

It had taken only a few minutes for Ensign Eric Lingard to fly from Chatham Naval Air Station to Nauset Beach, but Orleans resident Leon Ellis was among those hoping help might have come sooner.

"The thing that impresses us most," snapped Ellis, "was the length of time which elapsed before the first plane arrived."

Under the circumstances, however, the flying boat made great time. It reached the beach at 10:58 a.m.—just thirty minutes after the submarine commenced its bombardment off Nauset Beach and less than ten minutes since the air station received word of the attack.

Captain Ainsleigh was among some who thought the plane was German. In fact, the quixotic Ainsleigh feared the aircraft had launched from inside the submarine and was working in concert with the *U-156* to help signal the range of the tug and barges.

Dr. Taylor reported the arrival of the plane to the *Boston Globe* with skepticism: "There is an airship hovering over the fight, but it seems to be doing nothing but looking on." Of course, from a distance, it was hard for the good doctor to really know what was happening.

From their seaplane, Lingard, Shields and Howard could see "smoke across the horizon [and] soon the flame of guns. Then…the outlines of the burning boats, one on end, another sinking and a big thing not five hundred yards off."

The "big thing" was none other than the *U-156*.

"The submarine was an immense one," said Shields. "It looked like a destroyer or a small cruiser, three hundred feet long at least."

From the bow of the plane, Howard thought the submarine's crew, who were donning white caps, blouses and dungarees, resembled American sailors. There were at least thirty of them running around the deck and working the guns.

Now confident that this was not another false alarm and that an enemy submarine was, in fact, shelling the coast, Ensign Lingard took a deep breath and prepared to bomb the raider that, as Shields recalled, was "blazing away complacently as if there was no air station with[in] a thousand miles."

Unfortunately for the crew of *U-156*, the cavalry had finally arrived.

As the aircraft swooped forward, Howard remained steady and waited for the perfect opportunity to release his one bomb.

"They did not appear to see us until we were almost upon them," remembered Shields. "As we nosed down toward them, there was a great deal of commotion and hustling around on deck. They then seemed in a Hell of a hurry to get away."

Howard lined his sight "dead on the deck" and pulled the release just eight hundred feet above the sub, defying instructions to bomb their target at a safe distance. But for some reason, the Mark IV bomb failed to drop.

Howard motioned with his hand for Lingard to circle around so that he could try to discharge the bomb a second time. Again, ignoring the "1,000-foot rule," Lingard and his crew flew just four hundred feet above the U-boat—so close that the bomb's explosion below would likely blow the men from their aircraft.

Again, the mechanic tried to discharge the bomb, but again the bomb release failed to cooperate. The release was then tested and determined to be stuck. Frustrated but not willing to throw in the towel just yet, Howard, clearly not a man afraid of heights, quickly jumped out of the cockpit and onto the plane's lower wing—a distance of six feet—before the target below their aircraft was

View of a submarine from the cockpit of a plane. *U.S. Navy*.

out of range. Lingard and Shields watched in disbelief as a blast of wind nearly sent their "fearless" mechanic tumbling into the ocean below, but much to his colleagues' amazement, Howard maintained his balance. Gripping the plane's strut with one hand and holding the bomb with the other, Howard took a deep breath, uncurled his fingers and released the Mark IV.

Howard's aim was immaculate, but frustratingly, the bomb failed to explode once it hit the sea, just a few feet from the sub. The airmen were dumbfounded. Had the bomb worked properly, the submarine would have likely been incapacitated or even destroyed.

"When that bomb failed us," Howard said, "it was the meanest disappointment a man could have! Lingard is the most wonderful pilot I ever rode with. He flew exactly over the center of the submarine [and we dropped the bomb] within a few feet of the submarine. If the bomb had functioned, the submarine would have been done for." Understanding the magnitude of the situation, the mechanic grumbled, "Lingard knew then that his one big chance at history had…slipped by."

Out of bombs and having missed an opportunity to sink the German submarine, Lingard contemplated flying his plane into the raider with the goal of disabling the U-boat. But Howard noted that this action, though heroic, would not have the desired effect. One wonders if they worried about their own fate had they followed through with Lingard's suggestion.

Having literally dodged a bullet, the *U-156* then aimed her deck guns at the annoying fly buzzing over her head. Not able to communicate through the engine noise, Shields hastily scribbled Lingard a note that read simply: "They are firing shrapnel."

At least three bursts of fire flew past the aviators, but none hit the plane. Lingard climbed high into the sky, with the hope of avoiding additional fire, and planned to track the submerging sub, still visible to the aviators above, until the air station sent additional planes—preferably planes with working bombs.

*** 

Captain Feldt and the crew of the *U-156* had a seemingly endless supply of ammunition, and without resistance from the airmen above, they continued to make short work of their prey.

Still on the phone with the *Globe*, Dr. Taylor updated the press: "They've set some of the barges afire with their explosive shells and the towboat is also done up. The U-boat has closed up considerably and seems to be between two of the remaining barges, firing as fast as he can."

One shell hit the boiler on *Barge 766*, the second barge in line, and the vessel soon exploded. Within minutes, the barge began to sink. The captain and crew of *Barge 703*, the third in line, barely had time to vacate their craft before a shell hit it amidship. Both crews escaped to their respective lifeboats unharmed.

Joseph Perry, who had been taking in the sun when the raider emerged from the depths, captained the last barge in the towline. His craft, *Barge 740*, was the *U-156*'s final target.

As soon as it became evident that his barge would be shelled, Perry shouted to his nephew John, "To the lifeboat, to the lifeboat! German submarines!"

The young deckhand spun in his shoes and raced toward the stern of the barge.

"John, it'll be us next!" Perry shouted as shells began to crash nearby.

"We received in turn a hail of shot." Perry later recalled. "Shells struck my craft in the bow. Each one just seemed to lift the deck clear."

The captain shoved his wife and eleven-year-old daughter, Minnie, into the barge's lifeboat and took off for the beach, but not before one of the shells exploded beneath the stern of his barge. A rain of seawater showered down on Perry and his family, threatening to swamp their raft. Perry's wife fainted, but no one on board was hurt.

Perry, like most Americans that day, was not impressed with the Germans' aim: "My Minnie could have done better."

After motoring the lifeboat "just a few rods" from the barge, her boiler exploded, and she sank within minutes. With shrapnel continuing to burst all around them, Perry "rowed like mad for the shore."

***

Meanwhile, Captain Tapley, Bogovich, Zitz and the other members of the *Perth Amboy* reached the beach at Station Number 40. They were met by a horde of beachgoers eager to lend a hand.

Pierce and his lifesavers arrived on shore around the same time. James Patrick McCue, a local doctor, was summoned to help the wounded sailors coming in from the surf. He looked over Bogovich, the bloodied helmsman, and his initial diagnosis was not good; Bogovich's arm was badly shattered between the elbow and the shoulder, and the lower third of the humerus had been completely torn out.

The doctor thought Bogovich might lose his hand or even his entire arm if something wasn't done quickly. McCue considered amputating the

*Above and opposite*: The *Perth Amboy*'s crew arrives on shore. *Courtesy of the Orleans Historical Society.*

*Above and next page*: Pierce, in the stern, and the surfmen from Station Number 40 arrive on shore. *Courtesy of the Orleans Historical Society.*

arm right there on the beach, but after a second look, he decided he might be able to save it. For the time being, all he could do was provide basic first aid and started by pouring iodine on the open wound. Bogovich, in turn, groaned in pain. The agony the helmsman endured, recalled a witness, was unforgettable.

Injured helmsman John Bogovich being transported from the beach. *Courtesy of the Orleans Historical Society.*

McCue treated Zitz next and decided it was best to take both of the men to his office to continue care, as there was only so much he could do on the beach. Before leaving, Dr. McCue declared, "Whoever put this tourniquet on this man saved him from bleeding to death." Number One Surfman Moore earned his pay that day.

Moore's commanding officer, Captain Pierce, breathed a sigh of relief and then turned his attention back toward the sea; the sailors aboard the tug's barges had all launched lifeboats and appeared to be en route to Nauset Beach, some two miles to the north.

\*\*\*

Word of mouth and the sound of gunfire had alerted townsfolk up and down Cape Cod's arm that a German U-boat was shelling the town of Orleans. Onlookers—some say hundreds, while others claim thousands—gathered to catch a glimpse of the menacing U-boat offshore.

As far away as Provincetown, a Captain Kendrick tried to solicit business by ferrying the curious out to the scene of the crime: "One dollar a round trip to see the submarine! See the enemy craft! Go and see the submarine!" Kendrick refused to refund patrons if the submarine submerged before they arrived.

Ten miles away, Walter Barr noticed commotion from his summer home in Chatham. "When we heard news, a party of cottagers started for Orleans to see the excitement," recalled Barr. Later, Barr and his band of vacationers would join the growing crowd on the shore and watch the show's final act.

Just a few miles from Nauset Beach, in downtown Orleans, Model-T Ford "Flivvers," some fender to fender, were streaming toward the coast. Eva Leslie Ellis turned to a friend and shook her head. "Look at all those fools going down to the beach to get shot at," she said.

In a letter written to his son Russell after the attack, Herbert R. Gills described "people…thronging in automobiles and on foot" who had converged on the bluffs and on the beach.

One young man described the scene as one that contained a "carnival spirit."

In a nearby cellar, excited children hid their heads and shrieked after the sound of each report but lifted them once the danger passed.

One father confidently reassured his terrified daughter, "You'll be all right—you're with me."

In another seaside home, one horrified and apparently confused woman cowered in the corner and cried, "I don't mind dying, but I'd hate to be killed."

Some used opera glasses to get a better view, but as the *Boston Post* noted, the cottagers "did not have to move to see every detail of the little drama. No moving picture manager could have staged a sea battle more effectively for the thousands of summer visitors in this vicinity. Bathers taking their morning dip scurried ashore when shells splashed within a few hundred yards of them and watched the German exhibition of frightfulness without fear, but with keen excitement from the beach."

One bystander was more direct: "We weren't scared, we were mad!"

While some simply watched from afar, other onlookers were willing to lend a hand to their compatriots who were paddling furiously toward the beach.

With the surfmen from Station Number 40 preoccupied helping the crew of the *Perth Amboy*, Captain Frank Freeman, a deaf lobsterman, took the towlines from barges *766* and *703* and used the motor from his skiff to expedite their exodus to shore.

Meanwhile, the privately owned *Ina* came alongside Perry's lifeboat, about a half mile from shore, and towed his family to safety.

Lou Delano, who earlier had been walking to town to get the Sunday paper with his father, noticed how a woman emerging from one of the

One of the tug's lifeboats being towed to shore. *Courtesy of the Orleans Historical Society.*

lifeboats was less concerned with the dangers around her than with what she was wearing in public. As she stepped out of the dory, she immediately began to lament "that she was in a house dress and had not time to change."

Others who reached the beach safely joined the Ainsleigh family in celebration. Some dropped to their knees and kissed the sand.

With refugees now streaming ashore, Dr. Taylor decided it was time to hang up with the *Globe* and rushed to the beach to assist the wounded. After all, he was a physician, not a reporter. At first glance, Captain Ainsleigh seemed to need the most medical attention among the bargemen, but his wounds appeared worse than they really were; an ill-placed bandage on his right arm had failed to stanch the loss of blood. Below that bandage, a tiny piece of metal had opened a vein. Once Dr. Taylor placed his trained hands on the captain, he appeared little worse for the wear. "They are not serious," Taylor predicted. "The wounds are in the fleshy parts of the forearms and will soon be all right."

Taylor ushered the other cold, distraught seamen back to his home, which was already filled with neighbors and strangers alike. Later, Taylor described the cottage as "something like a Red Cross station, a home for the destitute and a club all in one."

***

The Chatham Naval Air Station had suffered a number of setbacks since first receiving word of the submarine attack. It seemed everything that could go wrong, did go wrong. This was unacceptable because the base had been built to thwart far-reaching threats like German U-boats.

At 11:04 a.m., the station's commander, Captain Eaton, returned to the air station, having ended a five-hour search for the blimp that had gone missing days earlier. Shortly thereafter, he was briefed on the seemingly unbelievable situation going on offshore. The commander knew the station was short on planes, so he decided to take matters into his own hands. At 11:15 a.m., forty-five minutes after the *U-156*'s attack began, Captain Eaton took off in an R-9 seaplane—number 991—in an effort to personally sink the German raider.

The R-9, also built by Curtiss Aeroplane and Motor Company, had been built specifically to combat enemy submarines. But unlike the HS-1L flying boat, it could carry two Mark IV bombs. However, usually only one was carried in an effort to keep the weight down, which was the case that day. As the pilot, Eaton usually flew the seaplane from the front cockpit while his bomber sat in the back. On July 21, 1918, however, Eaton was flying solo.

R-9 seaplane. *Courtesy of the San Diego Air & Space Museum.*

Approximately five minutes later, Reuben Hopkins, still in the lookout tower at Coast Guard Station Number 40, turned his head to the southwest to see Eaton's plane flying "right out, straight over the bluff, in a bee-line for the sub."

Ensign Lingard, who had been tracking and circling the sub—all the while evading antiaircraft fire—greeted the arrival of the captain's seaplane with renewed vigor: "[It was] the prettiest sight I ever hoped to see. Right through the smoke of the wreck, over the lifeboats and all, here came Captain Eaton's plane, flying straight for the submarine, and flying low. He saw [the submarine's] high-angle gun flashing, too, but he came ahead."

Lingard hoped his commanding officer would succeed where he and his colleagues had failed and deliver a decisive blow to the raider below.

"As I bore down upon the submarine, it fired," said Eaton, "I zigzagged and dove as it fired again."

The raider's guns blasted at least four rounds into the sky as Eaton advanced, but the shrapnel missed the seaplane. Despite the fire, Eaton was determined to get his plane positioned over the raider in order to hit his target. Glancing below, he seemed to have arrived just in time. "They were getting under way and scrambling down the hatch when I flew over them and dropped my bomb," recalled Eaton.

At 11:22 a.m., Eaton, also ignoring the "1,000-foot rule," bombed the Germans from a height of just five hundred feet. He braced for the explosion, but instead Eaton's payload splashed one hundred feet from the sub—a dud. "Had the bomb functioned, the submarine would have literally been smashed," Eaton lamented.

Enraged and frustrated, Eaton reportedly grabbed a monkey wrench from a toolbox inside his cockpit and hurled it at the Germans. Still not content, Eaton then dumped the rest of the plane's tools—as well as the metal toolbox—over the side with the hopes of at least giving one of the German sailors a concussion. Those on the sub, in turn, thumbed their noses at the paper tiger in the sky.

The raider had lucked out so far, but the crew of the *U-156* had no idea that the airplanes circling above their submersible were out of bombs. The next Mark IV dropped from the sky could destroy the sub, and other planes might soon be on their way. Captain Feldt decided it was finally time to head back out to sea, and at approximately 11:25 a.m., he ordered his raider to dive.

From the HS-1L, Ensign Shields described the hurried action below: "The gun nearest the conning tower disappeared in the deck…it appeared they did not have time to put all the guns away before they started to submerge."

Sensing the submarine was on the move, Lingard, Shields and Howard flew off to alert other seafaring vessels that an enemy raider was on the prowl. Meanwhile, Eaton continued to circle the U-boat to keep it in his sights until additional planes arrived. However, the late morning fog and the smoke from the guns made his task difficult. The *U-156* began to steam south, out toward sea, zigzagging as she went. Then, like a magician, she disappeared underneath the surface behind a cloud of smoke.

Captain Eaton breathed a sigh of relief. Although the bombs dropped from the sky had failed to detonate, perhaps his planes had at least hastened the sub's exit.

***

From the watchtower at Station Number 40, Reuben Hopkins also breathed a sigh of relief. The ocean in front of him was calm once again, save for the bubbles rising from where the U-boat had submerged.

However, Hopkins's respite was short-lived.

Approximately five minutes later, the *U-156* surfaced again. This time her hull was perpendicular to the beach, and her deck guns faced Station Number 40.

For an hour, the station had been a silent observer to the battle being waged offshore, but now it appeared as if Hopkins would experience the all mighty power of the German guns. Caught like a deer in headlights, Hopkins "had a great urge to head for the stairs," but he did not leave his post. Instead, he simply stared. "The crew of the submarine started to elevate their gun," he recalled, "and I realized I was looking down its muzzle, which gave me mixed feelings. However, I reflected it had taken three shots to hit the tug—I would give them one and then decide what to do next. I saw a flash and heard the shot scream past, just east of my tower window."

The shell landed in a tidal estuary behind the surf station known locally as "The River."

Hopkins and the surf station were spared. By noon, the U-boat had submerged once again. This time, it was for good. Hopkins could finally relax. Later, he would categorize the incident as "one of the most thrilling sights I have ever seen."

Just after noon, the First Naval District in Boston relayed a report of the attack to Washington, D.C.: "The Navy Department at noon received a dispatch from the First Naval District stating that Coast Guard Station 40 at Orleans, Mass, on the coast between Cape Cod and Chatham, Mass, reports sighting a tug on fire and three barges* being shelled by a submarine."

---

* Again, there were four barges, not three, as initially reported.

At around the same time, another R-9 seaplane from Chatham Naval Air Station arrived off the beach and dropped a Mark IV bomb on what the pilot thought was a periscope poking out from the surf. Whether the aviator spied the submarine or not was inconsequential because his bomb also failed to detonate. Out of munitions and having apparently missed the show, the seaplane flew back to the air station.

## ATTACK ON ORLEANS TIMELINE

| EVENT | TIME |
|---|---|
| *Perth Amboy* passes Nauset Beach Light Station | 10:15 a.m. |
| *U-156* begins shelling *Perth Amboy* and her four barges | *10:29 a.m. |
| Captain Robert Pierce calls Chatham Naval Air Station (CNAS) and reports attack | 10:40 a.m. |
| Lieutenant (JG) Elijah E. Williams hears the bombardment seven miles away at the CNAS | 10:48 a.m. |
| Lieutenant Williams sounds the alarm and orders planes into air | 10:49 a.m. |
| CNAS receives Captain Pierce's call (lost ten minutes in transmission) | 10:50 a.m. |
| HS-1L 1693 attempts to take off but cannot due to a spark plug problem | 10:50 a.m. |
| HS-1L 1695, with Lingard, Shields and Howard, takes off from CNAS | 10:54 a.m. |
| Dr. J. Danforth Taylor calls the *Boston Globe* | *10:55 a.m. |
| HS-1L 1695 arrives off Nauset Beach in Orleans | 10:58 a.m. |
| Captain Eaton ends the search for the missing blimp and returns to CNAS | 11:04 a.m. |
| Captain Eaton, in R-9 991, takes off from CNAS | 11:15 a.m. |
| R-9 991 drops a Mark IV bomb on the *U-156* | 11:22 a.m. |
| *U-156* submerges | 11:25 a.m. |
| *U-156* surfaces | *11:30 a.m. |
| *U-156* submerges again and disappears out to sea | 11:45 a.m. to 12:00 p.m. |
| A second R-9 from CNAS drops a Mark IV bomb on a "periscope" | 12:00 p.m. |

*approximate time

The crew of the *Perth Amboy* safely on shore. *From the collection of William P. Quinn.*

Finally, after an hour and a half, the Attack on Orleans was over. During that time, nearly 150 rounds had been fired by the *U-156*—an average of more than one every minute. The attack was like nothing the inhabitants of Orleans had ever experienced before. At first, the men kept their wives away from the beach in an effort to shield them from the supposed blood and gore. Rumors ran wild that someone had been killed, that others had been wounded and that at least one sailor might be missing. In spite of this, women, along with their children, were soon bounding down the bluffs, hoping to meet the sailors who had come in from the surf.

The survivors were treated like celebrities and hailed as heroes for beating, or at least surviving, the German onslaught. Children, in particular, enjoyed the show, and many flocked to the two Ainsleigh boys. Young Jack was regaled for flying the Stars and Stripes in the face of the enemy, while others rushed to shake the hand of his older brother, Charles, the young man who *might* have fired his rifle at the German sailors. After greeting the elder Ainsleigh boy with a hearty shake, one admiring tyke claimed he'd never wash his hand again.

After receiving medical treatment, Captain Ainsleigh wandered the beach in search of his loyal confidant, Rex, who he had not seen since hastily evacuating the barge. Ainsleigh called out his name but unfortunately had no luck locating the family collie. "I am very sorry for my dog," said

Brothers Jack and Charles Ainsleigh after the attack. *From the collection of William P. Quinn.*

Ainsleigh. "We were unable to get him off into the powerboat. He was a great companion of my wife and two sons."

Although the planes from the air station had had a terrible morning, at least they had given a counterattack a try. Ships from the U.S. Navy, stationed in Provincetown, had not even bothered to show up. Those on shore directed their attention to Major Clifford Harris, the local commander of the state guard and one of the few men of uniform, who by now had his troops assembled on the beach.

"The people down here were pretty well wrought up about not getting any assistance from the Provincetown naval station," Harris recalled.

Despite the navy's absence, the major was confident that he and his men were ready to repel a German invasion. With rifles at the ready, the soldiers had strategically positioned themselves behind a row of automobiles in the bluffs above the beach. Each man was ready, willing and able to do whatever was necessary to keep the enemy from reaching shore.

\*\*\*

That afternoon, the surfmen of Station Number 40 rowed back out to the scene of the crime to check on the condition of the smoldering tug, which miraculously remained afloat. This time, Reuben Hopkins was among the assigned crew. He noted the many shell holes on the side of the *Perth Amboy* but despite the damage declared the tug seaworthy. Three of the four barges, on the other hand, had disappeared. Only Captain Ainsleigh's *Lansford* remained somewhat afloat.

"The only unusual thing we saw during the trip out and back," noted Hopkins, "was a bedraggled hen, floating freely in a coop, evidently from the deck of one of the barges."

The *Lansford* after the attack. *From the collection of William P. Quinn.*

Walter Eldridge, a Chatham fisherman and one of the many locals who flocked to the beach that morning to lend a hand, also launched his skiff in the direction of the flotsam offshore. Among the debris, Eldridge spied a collie struggling bravely in the sea. Rex "met him with yelps of joy as he approached the hull."

Once on shore, Rex dashed across the sand and met his delighted master, Captain Ainsleigh. The collie was not the only animal that managed to get away from the ark unharmed. One of the Ainsleighs' "bedraggled hens" also escaped her coop and made it to shore. Young Jack, whose fifteen minutes of fame had recently expired, seized the hen and tucked it under his arm. With the help of the local children on the beach, he proceeded to build a makeshift coop with some of the wood from the barges tumbling in on the waves.

\*\*\*

In the early afternoon, the ever-defiant Eric Lingard flew a second sortie over the waters off Orleans with the goal of finding his adversary. Ensign Shields once again accompanied him. During the flight, the aviators spied an oil slick. Thinking the submarine was submerged just below the surface, Lingard's plane released another Mark IV bomb into the ocean—the fourth dropped by the air station that day. It, too, failed to explode.

\*\*\*

As the afternoon ticked away, Dr. James McCue continued to treat the injuries of John Bogovich and John Zitz back in the comfort of his office. There was still talk of Bogovich losing his right hand, and McCue could only do so much from his office on the Cape. He decided it was best to rush the injured helmsman and his shipmate by train to Massachusetts General Hospital in Boston. While recording routine information from his patient, McCue became suspicious when Zitz offered up two last names: Zitz and Evancih. In addition, Zitz had an accent and spoke with broken English. There were plenty of immigrants working on ships, but something about this sailor's accent raised an alarm. Inquiring further, McCue learned that Bogovich was not an American either. The two injured seamen sitting in the doctor's office hailed from Austria.

An ally of Germany and a member of the Central powers, the Austro-Hungarian Empire in 1918 was at war with the United States. One of the first two belligerents of the war, the "Dual Monarchy" had been ravaged by four years of carnage; nearly 1.5 million of its citizens had perished in battles against the Russians, Serbians and Italians. It was the assassination of the Austrian-Hungarian archduke, Franz Ferdinand, in Sarajevo in the summer of 1914 that had started the war, so the empire had a reason to fight. But after bearing witness to the slaughter of its youth for the past four years, it desperately wanted to get out of the war. The Germans, however, would not stand for it. Old alliances ran too deep.

The United States had been at war with the Austro-Hungarian Empire since December 7, 1917, but the two countries spent little time firing shots at each other on the battlefield. Now, with the war going poorly and backed into a corner, could Germany's closest ally be sending agents of espionage to infiltrate America's shore? Might these agents be working in concert with the German submarines?

As word of the attack continued to spread up and down the arm of Cape Cod, rumors flourished, and residents appeared on edge. German-phobia, already heightened, was now in overdrive. Nervous Cape Codders began seeing the Hun everywhere.

Passengers aboard a train traveling to Boston that afternoon reported seeing two surfaced submarines off the coast of Wellfleet, which sits on the Cape's "wrist." The sailors on the sub appeared to be smoking cigarettes or cigars and, according to those on the train, apparently "looked like Germans." What it means to be "German-looking" is certainly up for debate, but it is doubtful the sailors donned spiked helmets atop their heads.

Sometime after the attack, there were wild rumors that German sailors had crept ashore and surreptitiously taken in a movie in Boston. Other versions of the story suggested the Germans went to shore in Provincetown or in nearby Beverly. Some locals even claimed that German spies had infiltrated the Chatham Naval Air Station and had tampered with the plane's bombs, thus explaining the failures experienced by the aviators that morning.

While there was little truth to any of this scuttlebutt, residents, including Dr. McCue, were not taking any chances. German skullduggery was legendary, and nothing out of the ordinary should be taken for granted. The doctor conferred with the deputy sheriff to determine what should be done with the suspicious Austrians. Not able to come to a resolution, they then rendezvoused with Lieutenant Elijah Williams from the air station, but it seemed as if no one was certain what should be done. Eventually, orders were issued by someone from the Intelligence Department to hold the Austrians incommunicado pending an investigation into their presence aboard the tug. In the meantime, American courtesy prevailed, at least for the time being, and the shipmates were soon on their way via train to the hospital in Boston.

By then, the *Boston Globe*, thanks to Dr. Taylor's scoop, was running a story in its evening edition on the submarine attack. Later, a gracious editor sent

Dr. Taylor $150 and a box of Corona cigars as a show of thanks. The good doctor, who did not smoke, gave most of them away.

Eager to catch up, other dailies scrambled their reporters to Cape Cod. Soon the sandy roads that snaked their way to Nauset Beach were crammed with newsmen en route to interview survivors of the attack and dig up any gossip they deemed fit to print.

Bogovich and Zitz reached Boston by train shortly after 9:00 p.m. and were whisked away to the hospital. The press rushed the two Austrians hoping for an interview, but Bogovich, still in severe pain and barely conscious, was able to provide only a few pithy quotes.

Hoping for the juiciest of details, reporters then turned their attention to any other passengers returning from a weekend on the Cape. Everyone who departed the train, it seemed, had something to say, and the following day, newspapers across America would document the "Attack on Orleans" to their readers. Still, many questions remain unanswered: Why had the bombs dropped by the air station failed to detonate? And why had the German raider attacked such a seemingly worthless target as a tugboat and barges in the first place? These questions would eventually be answered, but for the time being, the residents of Orleans kept a cautious eye on the sea. The World War had finally come to the American mainland.

Just off Nauset Beach, the *Perth Amboy* smoldered well into the night, a warm orange glow still visible to the curious who wandered the beach.

Still, she refused to sink.

# ATTACK ON ORLEANS

## LOCATION OF PARTICIPANTS DURING THE ATTACK ON ORLEANS

### The German submarine *U-156*
Captain Richard Feldt

### The *Rose*
Captain Marsi Schuill

### Nauset Beach
Dr. Joshua Danforth Taylor (called the *Boston Globe* and treated Captain Ainsleigh)
Major Clifford Harris (local battalion commander of the state guard)

*Lansford* (first barge in tow)
Captain Charles Ainsleigh
Mrs. Ainsleigh (wife)
Charles D. Ainsleigh (son)
Jack Ainsleigh (son)
Rex (dog)
unnamed hen

*Barge 766* and *Barge 703*

*Barge 740* (last barge in tow)
Captain Joseph Perry
Virginia Perry (wife)
Minnie Perry (daughter)
John Leighton (nephew)

### U.S. Coast Guard Station No. 40
Captain Robert F. Pierce (keeper)
William D. Moore (number one surfman)
Reuben Hopkins (signalman in watchtower)

*Perth Amboy* (tug)
Captain James.P. Tapley
John Bogovich
John Zitz
+ thirteen other crewmen

Dr. James Patrick McCue (treated Bogovich and Zitz)

## Chatham Naval Air Station
Captain Philip B. Eaton (commander, R-9 pilot)
Lieutenant (JG) Elijah E. Williams (executive officer)
Ensign Eric A. Lingard (HS-1L 1695 pilot)
Ensign Edward M. Shields (HS-1L 1695 assistant pilot)
Chief Special Mechanic Edward H. Howard (HS-1L 1695 observer)

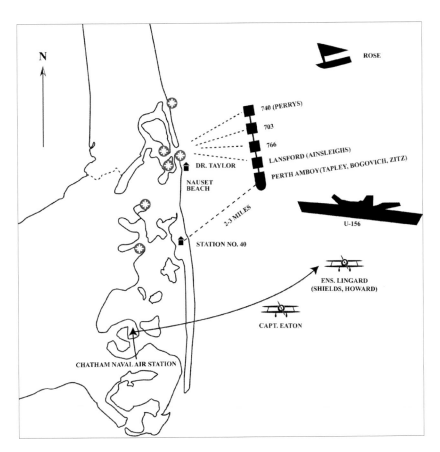

Map of the Attack on Orleans. *Chuck Kacsur.*

# CHAPTER 7

# SHELLSHOCKED

*It is more or less in the nature of a circus stunt done also to impress the German people...*
*—Rear Admiral Spencer S. Wood*

On July 22, 1918, newspapers all over the Northeast gave the *U-156*'s raid on Cape Cod front-page treatment, and the Attack on Orleans immediately became a media sensation.

The *Boston Globe*, thanks largely to Dr. Taylor's scoop, ran the masthead, "GERMAN SUBMARINE SINKS THREE BARGES."

The *New York Times* reported, "U-BOAT GIVES NO WARNING; Women and Children Shelled in Barges; One Man Loses an Arm." Bogovich, of course, had not lost his arm and was still recovering at Mass General.

"American Coast Is Attacked for First Time in Century," read another headline.

As they fingered through the dailies, Americans slowly began to understand the gravity of the raid: "When shells from the German submarine were fired at the *Perth Amboy* yesterday and struck the soil of Cape Cod, they broke a record of more than 100 years' standing. It was the first time in that interval that any foreign power had fired upon our coast."

Other newspapers expressed distaste and bemusement toward the Germans in the bodies of their stories. The *Boston Post* exclaimed, "The Hun showed himself in his true colors when without warning he shelled totally defenseless craft carrying men and women engaged in peaceful pursuits." The *Provincetown Advocate* stated sarcastically that "Kaiser Wilhelm's navy scored a glorious victory off Orleans."

The *Boston Post*'s July 22, 1918 headline. *Courtesy of the Orleans Historical Society.*

The *Boston Globe* even ran a cartoon that lampooned the actions taken by the German navy by depicting Kaiser Wilhelm exulting in a victory over an "empty coal barge."

But the raid was no laughing matter. The day after the Attack on Orleans, President Woodrow Wilson ordered the federal government to take control of the Cape Cod Canal from the Boston, Cape Cod and New York Canal Company to ensure the protection of shipping along New England's coast. Administered by the Federal Railroad Administration, ships could now use the canal without paying a toll. The government also announced it would dredge the canal to a depth of twenty-five feet, enabling larger boats passage. Had the government done this sooner, as it had done with other waterways on the East Coast, the *Perth Amboy* and the four barges might never have been fired on by a German U-boat.

Meanwhile, off the coast of Nauset Beach, the *Perth Amboy* was still smoldering, much to the excitement of the onlookers who continued to converge on the bluffs and on the shoreline. Salvage crews arrived on scene later in the day and eventually extinguished the flames. Once the smoke cleared, it was determined that the tugboat was, in fact, still salvageable. The hull was visibly scarred as a result of taking the brunt of the *U-156*'s wrath, but remarkably there was little damage done below the *Perth Amboy*'s

The *Perth Amboy*'s burned-out engine room. *Courtesy of Richard M. Boonistar.*

The *Perth Amboy* smolders while the *Lansford* bobs in the background. *From the collection of William P. Quinn.*

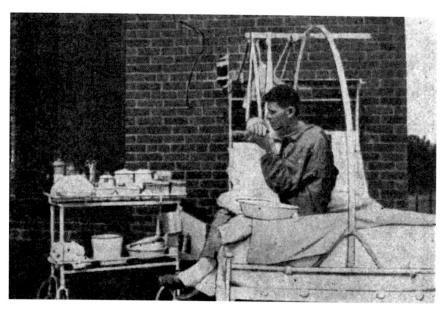

John Bogovich recovering at Massachusetts General Hospital. *From the* New England Journal of Medicine.

waterline. Workers clipped the steel tow cable at the stern of the tug that was connected to the waterlogged *Lansford*, which still bobbed partly submerged below the surface, and then prepared to tow it to the town of Vineyard Haven on nearby Martha's Vineyard.

When the famous tugboat arrived in port, Captain James Tapley and his boat were given, as Tapley recalled, a "grand reception" and greeted by whistles and gongs from patriotic islanders. Although the ship was noticeably damaged, the *Perth Amboy* would survive to tug again another day.

At Massachusetts General Hospital, *Perth Amboy* crew members John Bogovich and John Zitz continued to recover from their respective injuries.

In broken English, Bogovich recalled what happened twenty-four hours earlier: "I was at the wheel steering when they came. One-two-three. I do not know what you call them… bullets? I fell, what you say, in the faint. When they helped me into the little boat I saw what hit me—the submarine."

Despite their ethnicity, it was determined that neither of the Austrians had anything to do with the attack. To reporters, Bogovich protested how he had moved to the United States before the war and had no interest in harming the country he now called home: "I come here six years ago for I did not want to go into service, and now they get me with bullets."

At the hospital, doctors took X-rays of Bogovich's arm and shoulder, which indicated a substantial piece of shell was still embedded in his body. Once anesthetized, a three-quarter-inch cube of metal was plucked from the helmsman's back. Additional shell fragments and bone were taken from his right arm. After

An X-ray showing Bogovich's shattered humerus. *From the* New England Journal of Medicine.

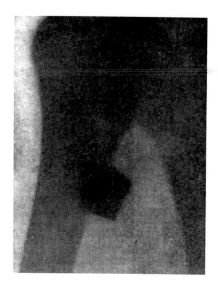

Shell fragment in Bogovich's left shoulder. *From the* New England Journal of Medicine.

everything was removed, doctors began the tedious task of cleaning and dressing his wounds. They were confident that Bogovich would not lose his arm, as was initially suspected.

\*\*\*

The Ainsleigh family, who had lost essentially all their possessions with the sinking of the *Lansford*, were quartered by the warm-hearted residents of Orleans.

"The neighbors at Nauset Harbor were very kind to us, and I can't thank the summer people half enough for their considerable treatment," said Captain Ainsleigh. However, the captain remained visibly shaken as a result of the attack and was described by his hosts as "a nervous wreck." He remained that way for the rest of his stay.

Young Jack Ainsleigh's hen, it turned out, would have her own fifteen minutes of fame. Children from the bluff took the hen and her makeshift coop and hid it inside an old barn. Outside, the young entrepreneurs built a sign that read: "See the hen that the Hun didn't get. Ten cents." Years later, one of the children, now fully grown, boasted, "You would be surprised at the number of people who paid us ten cents to see that hen. We children thought what a wonderful time we'd have with all the candy that ten cents would bring."

But sadly, it was not to be. When adults caught wind of this little moneymaking scheme, the funds were confiscated and donated to the Red Cross.

Youngsters were not the only ones seizing an opportunity to make a buck. Even the surfmen from Station Number 40 got in on the action. On the morning after the attack, the waves that lapped up against the beach were filled with debris, and sensing the historical magnitude of the attack, everyone in town seemed to want a piece of driftwood. As they had done for hundreds of years, "beachcombers" emerged and almost immediately began to scour the sands in search of souvenirs. A few business-savvy lifesavers sold pieces of wood from the barges that allegedly had washed up on shore. By the second week of August, they were running out of mementos, so one of

Debris from the barges on Nauset Beach. *Courtesy of Richard M. Boonistar.*

the surfmen took a Lyle gun* and aimed it at an old wooden hatch cover. The result? Instant souvenirs!

Splinters from one of the barges were one thing, but more coveted were fragments of shells fired by the German U-boat. Most of the raider's shells splashed harmlessly into the sea, but an unknown number—at least one, maybe two and perhaps as many as six—landed somewhere on the shore on Nauset Bar, Barley Neck or in Meeting House Pond. If souvenir hunters were lucky, they just might find a piece of one hidden in the sand or buried deep within the muck of the marsh. Apparently, they were not hard to come by. Elmer Snow, a cottager who had "witnessed the shelling from beginning to end," said, "That night [after the attack] about everyone in town had a piece of a shell." One of the lucky ones, Captain Frank Freeman, collected a shell fragment with dimensions that measured four and a half inches by two and a half inches.

Shortly after the attack, Frederick W. Snow, among others, lobbied Massachusetts senator Henry Cabot Lodge to have the U.S. Navy dig up an intact shell rumored to exist in the marsh below the bluffs and present it to the town of Orleans as a memorial; however, this idea never came to fruition.

Later in the week, some souvenirs from the Attack on Orleans were auctioned off in Martha's Vineyard, where the *Perth Amboy* was still

---

* A Lyle gun, also known as a line-throwing gun, was used to fire a rope in the direction of someone in distress.

Frank Freeman's shell fragment. *Courtesy of Richard M. Boonistar.*

undergoing repair. German shrapnel apparently "sold high, but battered bread pans could be bought for as little as 75 cents per piece." The tug's coffee pot was sold to a summer resident who used it to make coffee in the auction hall and, in turn, toasted the Allied cause. The funds accrued, like those generated from viewing Jack Ainsleigh's famous hen, were also given to the Red Cross.

In some instances, souvenirs were discovered by sheer chance. A week after the attack, Albert Herbert Moulton was casting for striped bass in the waters off Nauset Beach and accidentally hooked one of Chatham Naval Air Station's Mark IV bombs. Although it hit the sea as a dud, one would hope the angler exercised caution while reeling it to shore. Years later, Moulton sold the bomb to a neighbor, who fashioned it into a weathervane.

But not everyone was taking the attack so lightly. Fearing additional assaults by sea were inevitable, Major Clifford Harris, the local commander of the state guard, wrote to someone in Washington, D.C., and requested they send a piece of artillery to his beachside home, which he planned to mount in his yard that overlooked the sea.

The major's request was eventually denied.

The U.S. Navy, on the other hand, did send equipment to Cape Cod. Assuming the Cape's "elbow" was the new hot spot in the war on submarines, the navy had the Curtiss Aeroplane and Motor Company ship ten additional HS-2L flying boats to the air station. Cousins to the HS-1L, the newer 2Ls had bigger rudders and a greater wingspan, allowing it to carry larger, heavier bombs.

In addition, newly modified Davis guns also found their way to Chatham, and by the end of August, every flying boat was equipped with one. The Davis gun

gun was similar to a small cannon and fired six-pound projectiles that were capable of rendering a U-boat useless. At worst, they were far more reliable than the Mark IV bombs, which were also soon bound for the air station, though many wondered whether more bombs would even make a difference.

Local taxpayers were livid. The air base had cost millions of dollars and had been built specifically to combat submarines, yet the planes and pilots that were scrambled to come to Cape Cod's aid had failed in their objective. Some spread rumors that Eric Lingard and the other pilots who responded to the attack were aviation students from the Chatham Training Grounds whose "payloads" were actually nothing more than sandbags, something that would have normally been dropped during practice runs. Another rumor alleged that Lingard's Austro-Hungarian heritage, on his mother's side, might have been a factor.

Rear Admiral Spencer S. Wood, commandant of the First Naval District, had jurisdiction over Chatham Naval Air Station. It was Wood who had brought Lingard to Chatham a year earlier when he was desperately searching for aviators for the station. The commandant knew he would take the heat for the air station's failures, and hours after the attack, Wood was already engaged in damage control: "I want to correct the impression, given currently by certain published stories, that the Chatham aircraft were late in getting to the scene of the attack or were not otherwise promptly on the job. They were there and dropped two bombs, the explosion of either one of which might have been effective in destroying the hostile craft."

However, a single question regarding the bombs remained: Why had the Mark IVs dropped by Chatham's planes failed to explode? The press was already taking the U.S. Navy to task. Shortly after the attack, the *Boston Transcript* remarked, "It is reported that ammunition furnished in this district is notoriously unreliable…[T]his alone saved the enemy craft from destruction or from damage that would have made its capture easy."

Behind closed doors, the U.S. Navy began to take sweeping steps to ensure that tragic and embarrassing circumstances like this would never happen again. Munitions experts in the navy's Ordinance Bureau began inspecting its arsenal of Mark IVs to determine what the problem was. Surprisingly, these tests produced a "low percentage of failures." Still, pilots at Chatham who actually practiced dropping these bombs knew the Mark IVs were faulty. In the month before the Attack on Orleans, the air station dropped fifteen different Mark IVs during various tests, none of which exploded. Miraculously, the Chatham Naval Air Station even informed the Ordinance Bureau about this problem ahead of time, but in the epitome of what is surely a bureaucratic failure, these memos fell on deaf ears and went unanswered.

This was not simply a problem exclusive to Chatham. Said an officer from New York's Rockaway Naval Air Station, "We had a great deal of trouble with bombs supplied by the Ordnance Department. It was always a gamble whether they would explode when dropped. The affair at Chatham…was a glaring example of the unreliability of the fuse mechanisms."

An aviator attached to the Ordnance Bureau went even further, stating, "There was a great deal of question at all these stations as to whether the Mark IV would go off or not, and I was out to show them that it would. This was rather a difficult job because everyone in the department felt certain that the Mark IV was a failure."

In the end, munitions gurus determined that the "Mark IV bomb is an efficient bomb when properly cared for and properly operated, but that its mechanism is too complicated for the average personnel in whose charge it is placed." The Ordnance Department then decided to take steps to increase the likelihood the bombs would explode on future runs. "The performance of this bomb in service has shown that a simpler design is necessary," the U.S. Navy suggested, "and the Bureau inaugurated plans for a new design upon the failure of the first bombs."

Despite the bombs' obvious failures, Lieutenant Elijah Williams was quick to give kudos to his fellow aviators for chasing the *U-156* away from shore. He also went so far to credit the station's seaplanes for saving that part of Cape Cod. "It is reasonably certain," Williams said, "had the U-boat not been attacked from the air, she would have destroyed Chatham and Orleans not because of any possible military value, but for the decided moral effect that such destruction would have had." He added, "What a nice breakfast story this would have given the German newspapers—'Two American cities destroyed by U-boat.'"

Williams's imagination might have got the best of him, but his intentions were sincere.

"The 'Chatham Navy,'" a fellow aviator boasted, "invites the Germans to return."

There was, of course, one last question on the minds of everyone on Cape Cod: Why had a German U-boat bothered to attack a seemingly worthless target like the *Perth Amboy* and her barges in the first place? The nature and execution of the Attack on Orleans was quite different than any raid made by other submarines during the war and unlike any made by the *U-156* prior to July 21, 1918. The *U-156* fired an extraordinary amount of ammunition for any quarry, which was even more remarkable in the strange case of

One of Chatham Naval Air Station's R-9 seaplanes resting on Nauset Beach in the days after the attack. *Courtesy of the Tenney family.*

Orleans given the U-boat's targets: a steel towboat and four wooden barges, one of which was filled with harmless stones and three of which were devoid of any goods altogether.

Granted, the sailors on the submarine would not have known the barges were empty at the time, but assuming they were full, the mariners must have expected them to be filled with something worthwhile—something they could not resist turning their guns on. Given the amount of ammunition the raiders expended on the vessels, perhaps they suspected that President Wilson himself was aboard.

Many assumed the *U-156* had simply made a mistake. The *J.B. King* and the *Arlington* were two colliers that had passed by the "elbow" of Cape Cod earlier in the morning. Perhaps, in the confusion of the mid-morning haze, the raider mistook the *Perth Amboy* and her barges for one of these larger, more important vessels.

Captain Ainsleigh seemed to think so. "In my opinion, this U-boat… was lying in wait for something larger, but failing to find anything was determined to wreak vengeance upon us," Ainsleigh construed. "It is almost inconceivable to think that a German U-boat commander should attempt such an attack at this particular point, as it is only about 10 miles distance from Chatham and 25 miles in the other direction from Provincetown, where American submarines and destroyers have practice."

Others surmised that the *U-156* had surfaced off Nauset Beach to cut a transatlantic cable running from Brest, France, to Orleans. The theory was sound because the *U-151*, the super submarine that had wreaked havoc in the mid-Atlantic just one month earlier, had cut two similar cables off the coast of New York. In addition, the U.S. Navy had received intelligence that German submarines would target such cables, but it was never determined whether the *U-156* had a cable-cutting device. Hence, the theory remains just that—a theory.

Commandant Wood was quick to ridicule the German navy for attacking the irrelevant *Perth Amboy*, and in doing so, he probably hoped to take attention away from the failed Mark IV bombs. "The whole occurrence, from a strategic point of view, impressed me as a little short of ridiculousness," Wood said. "I gave the German government credit for having more sense than to waste good ammunition on a couple of scows worth hardly more than the ammunition that sank them, and believe the whole performance due to a desire to impress the American people with the nearness of the German operations and to excite pacifists, whom they think so numerous in this country, to renew their activities and end the war."

Wood hoped to rally the American people behind the government and paint the German attempts to intimidate Cape Cod as futile: "If the German sea-fighters are of the impression that these kinds of four-flush tactics will terrify the American people, they have still a lot to learn of the sentiment of this country."

Echoing Lieutenant Williams, Wood rendered the Attack on Orleans as a desperate attempt by the *U-156* to rally her homeland during the war's final hours: "It is more or less in the nature of a circus stunt done also to impress the German people with the idea that submarine warfare is being carried to the very shore of America and that the campaign of frightfulness is being waged relentlessly." Wood added, "Such foolish and futile demonstrations have quite the opposite effect, for they assure the [American] people rather than terrify them."

Captain Richard Feldt and the crew of the *U-156* probably paid little attention to the American spin. The *Perth Amboy* and her barges were notches on Feldt's belt—the latest in what he hoped would be many. While the U.S. Navy and American press tried to comprehend the magnitude of the Attack on Orleans, the raider turned its nose north and began to steam toward Nova Scotia. The captain had his orders; he and his crew had more ships to sink.

# CHAPTER 8

# THE FINAL CRUISE

*We want everything historical that we can get for Gloucester, and we want this.*
—*Asa G. Andrews*

On July 22, 1918, the day after she shelled the "elbow" of Cape Cod, the *U-156* spied the schooner *Robert and Richard*, which was returning to Gloucester, Massachusetts, with a cache of halibut. The submarine fired a single shot across the bow of the ship before the fishing boat slowed to a stop. The fishermen then filed out on deck with their hands in the air as a trio of Germans boarded the ship. Sensing his time had come, one of the fishermen asked the Germans what he intended to do with the crew. "Nothing," a German officer snapped. "You think too much of what [President] Wilson tells you."

The officer then demanded the ship's papers and flag (apparently as a memento), while other German sailors hastily placed a bomb below deck. The American fishermen were permitted to escape in a lifeboat unscathed, and soon the wooden schooner was on its way to the bottom of the sea.

Once again, the German U-boat got away. Americans continued to convey their disappointment with the way the government had handled its response to this new, foreign menace.

"The German submarines seemed to do as they pleased," penned a retired admiral in his memoirs.

"Once over here," added another naval commander, the submarines had "a fairly easy time of it."

# ATTACK ON ORLEANS

In an editorial that ran in the *Gloucester Times* less than one week after the Attack on Orleans, a writer noted how Germany's super submarine had become a game changer. No longer would the vast, seemingly endless Atlantic Ocean serve as a buffer against enemies from afar:

> *There was a time not so many months ago when Americans were thinking of the Great War as being 3,000 miles away, and therefore a contest from which they might entirely keep themselves free.*
>
> *But, since then distance has been abolished…We received last Sunday a very vivid reminder of the nearness of the battle when barges were sunk in sight of the summer residents of the town of Orleans.*
>
> *We know now if we never did before that no nation can live apart from others. And we who have thought ourselves safe from foreign entanglements do well to see how close this war has come to us. Victory is absolutely necessary.*

For the next month, the *U-156* continued to take aim at the North American fishing fleet and destroyed a whopping twenty-seven merchant ships. On August 26, after sinking the *Gloaming*, a Canadian fishing schooner, the *U-156* began her long journey home. Her American cruise was certainly something to marvel. Captain Feldt and his crew had destroyed forty-four ships in the western Atlantic. Regrettably, her cruise resulted in the deaths of twenty-two seamen—citizens from a variety of countries, including the six American sailors aboard the *San Diego*.

By autumn, the noose was closing in on the Central powers, and the Allies had gained the upper hand on both the western front and the war at sea. American and British ships sowed the waters around Europe, in particular the North Sea, with antisubmarine mines. The *U-156* had to run this gauntlet in order to return to her homeport. Up until now, the raider, having sailed on two successful cruises, had been lucky. But on September 25, her good fortune ran out. The *U-156* struck a mine somewhere off the coast of Norway and began to take on water. One account claims that all hands were lost at sea; another suggests that twenty-one of her sailors escaped to the Norwegian coast.

The fate of Captain Richard Feldt remains a mystery.

The *U-156* was the only super submarine dispatched to the western Atlantic that failed to return to Germany.

***

Back at the Chatham Naval Air Station, pilots continued to patrol the waters off Cape Cod. Reports of enemy submarines, almost all of them false, still trickled into the station throughout the summer and on into the fall.

On October 10, two weeks after the *U-156* was sunk, the Chatham Naval Air Station received an SOS from a South American liner that claimed to have sighted a U-boat.

Once again, a seaplane was scrambled to alert. On this occasion, Ensign Edward Shields, Eric Lingard's co-pilot during the Attack on Orleans, would be at the stick. Not wanting to miss an opportunity to destroy a U-boat, Lingard volunteered to serve as Shield's gunner. This time, their HS-1L flying boat was equipped with one of the station's new Davis guns, which had not been available during the *U-156*'s raid in July. Although still in its testing phase, the Davis gun, loaded with six-pound rounds and mounted on the bow of a seaplane, was determined to be an ideal weapon to combat enemy submarines.

Lingard and Shields left the air station at 11:45 a.m. and flew in the direction of the distressed steamer. The weather was gloomy but certainly nothing the airmen weren't accustomed to flying in. However, thirty-minutes after takeoff, a storm moved in. Forty-mile-per-hour winds began to rock the seaplane from side to side, and fifteen minutes later, a cracked cylinder forced

Davis gun mounted on the bow of a flying boat. *National Archives.*

Davis gun mounted on the bow of a flying boat. *U.S. Navy.*

the airmen to make an emergency landing at sea, thirty miles from shore. They landed safely, but soon heavy seas began to pummel their aircraft. The pilots knew that help would not be coming anytime soon. In fact, those back at the air station assumed that Shields, Lingard and the co-pilot, Ensign James Shilling, were probably dead—after all, it was October in the North Atlantic. For hours, the pilots did their best to stay warm and dry, but freezing waves mercilessly battered the stricken craft and soaked the aviators.

By 4:30 p.m., after four hours at sea, the flying boat slowly began to sink. To make matters worse, the sun would soon dip below the western horizon, and the temperature would surely drop. Too cold and weak to eat or drink,

Lingard and Shilling lay stretched on the wing throughout the night while waves continued to crash atop their already frozen backs. Meanwhile, Shields, having discovered a leak, ferociously bailed water from the cockpit. As the night wore on, Shilling dropped in and out of consciousness. Fearful he would slip into the sea and drown, Lingard crept from one side of the plane to the other and propped his friend farther up onto the wing, all while attempting to keep the wobbly wings of the flying boat level and above water.

Throughout the night and into the early morning, Lingard told stories and jokes to take his mind off the chill and to keep up the spirit of Shields. Shillings had by then fallen unconscious. The pilots knew it was only a matter of time before their flying boat dipped below the surface and sank to the bottom of the sea. The airmen would undoubtedly follow. In the meantime, all they could do was cling to their wrecked aircraft and pray for sunrise, calmer seas and rescue.

By dawn, the waves had thankfully subsided, and at 8:30 a.m., spirits rose when the frigid airmen spied four seaplanes flying overhead. Rescue would surely be imminent, they imagined. However, it would take another seven hours before the aviators were scooped from the sea by one of the navy's sub-chasers. Ensign Shillings, who was too weak to speak, was rescued first. Amazingly, just before they boarded the sub-chaser, Lingard and Shields dived back into the unforgiving Atlantic to retrieve their flying boat's Davis gun, which was required of airmen once their personal safety was assured.

All totaled, the three aviators had spent twenty-seven hours in the frigid Atlantic. Later, the station learned that the SOS call had been a false alarm; there were no German U-boats were in the area.

"Chatham was out of luck," quipped Lingard. "When the enemy came—no gun. When the [Davis] gun came—no enemy."

Shortly after returning to dry land, Eric Lingard developed pneumonia.[*] For the next two weeks, the "enthusiastic aviator," as he was described by one local paper, languished on a bed in the infirmary at the Chatham Naval Air Station, "patiently and bravely as a faithful warrior should without murmuring or complaint," according to the station's chaplain, Dr. Henry Van Dyke.

As Lingard's situation deteriorated, his sister, Olga, journeyed south from Annisquam to be alongside her brother, just as he had he been beside her when she had taken ill three years earlier at The Pines.

"War's over," Lingard whispered from his bed. "Don't care what the newspapers say—it's all over!"

---

[*] Lingard had pneumonia in 1907 as well.

Two days later, on the morning of October 29, 1918, Lingard took a turn for the worse. Fellow pilots crowding the infirmary choked back tears as they waited for news—Lingard was among the most-liked aviators at the station and a man they treasured as a friend.

Later that day, Dr. Van Dyke approached the crowd of mourners and reported the distressing news. "Early this morning," Dr. Van Dyke said, "one of your best comrades, a brave youth, a faithful officer, a daring and skillful aviator, passed out of this life. His death was the immediate consequence of injury and exposure which came to him in the course of duty as an air scout guarding the shores of our country."

Eric Adrian Alfred Lingard died just a week before his twenty-eighth birthday and less than two weeks before the end of the World War.

The *Boston Globe* reported the somber news in its obituary page, "Aviator Lingard Dead at Chatham: Intrepid Flyer Answered German U-boat Alarm."

Olga, of course, was devastated, but how her brother died caused her even more distress. "I cannot help being proud to have had so much to sacrifice," noted Olga, "but he did deserve the best death going—death by air or sea—a just climax to a life that had always been by the elements! And so my sorrow was bitter on his account when I saw his glorious personality being throttled by disease in a <u>bed</u>!"

"In my belief," Dr. Van Dyke countered, "Ensign Lingard died 'in the line of duty' and 'on the field of honor' as truly as anyone who fought in the trenches or on the high seas. He gave all that he had...Such a sacrifice is sure of its eternal reward. Let us stand still for a moment—in a silent prayer—in grateful memory of the courage, fidelity and devotion of Ensign Eric Lingard."

Although the air station had lost a handful of aviators (largely to accidents) during the World War, the death of Eric Lingard seemed to hit home. In a show of support, two hundred officers and men marched five miles from the air station to the funeral home to pay their last respects.

During the funeral, Lingard's old high school professor Frederick Winsor summed up his former student as "a lad who could get the best out of engine or man...an exhilarating companion, joyous and sympathetic. He hated show or sham, he went his own way among men, and he knew the true meaning of democracy."

It was a sentiment shared by many.

Ensign Shilling, who possibly owed his life to Lingard; Lieutenant Elijah Williams, the executive office of the air station; and another aviator accompanied Lingard's remains on the journey by train back to Annisquam, where he was buried with full military honors, his body dressed in the uniform of his rank, the gold service stripe of ensign on his sleeve. At the conclusion of the funeral, three volleys were fired by a rifle squad over the flag-draped casket before his remains were placed in the family tomb. Then, a bugler blew taps. Seaplanes from Chatham dropped garlands of flowers over Mount Adnah Cemetery as a final salute.

Somewhere, Eric Lingard was smiling.

\*\*\*

On May 25, 1919, long after the guns on the western front had fallen silent and the war had ended, Lieutenant Williams wrote to Olga and encouraged her to secure part of her brother's famous plane—the first to engage an enemy vessel in the western Atlantic—as a "historic relic." During the months following the end of the war, the Chatham Naval Air Station began to scrap its fleet of flying boats, which would soon become obsolete. Williams noted that Lingard's famous plane, number 1695, was "worn out in service…the hull only remains." If she hoped to secure the hull, Olga had to act fast; what was left of Lingard's plane had been relegated to the scrap heap and would soon be on its way to the Great Lakes Training School for "experimental purposes." If something were not done quickly, the remains of the famous plane would surely be lost to history.

In the weeks and months that followed, Olga, with the help of local politicians, petitioned the U.S. Navy to send 1695's hull to Gloucester.

"Lingard was a Gloucester boy…he gave his life in defense of the coast," noted Alderman Asa G. Andrews in an appeal to the navy. "We want everything historical that we can get for Gloucester, and we want this."

Lingard's hull being towed to Gloucester. *From the Cape Ann Shore.*

Lingard's hull being paraded through the city of Gloucester. *Gloucester Archives.*

Assistant Secretary of the Navy (and future president) Franklin D. Roosevelt apparently agreed. In a letter to Olga, Roosevelt wrote, "Knowing what a splendid young man your brother was, I can realize what a great loss you have suffered. Your brother lived up to the best traditions of the Navy, and I cannot speak too highly of his gallant work." As a result, Roosevelt ordered "that the hull of Seaplane 1695 be turned over to the Park Commissioners of Gloucester."

On July 3, 1919, the coveted hull was towed from Chatham to Gloucester by a sub-chaser. It was then turned over to the city officials and, in accordance with the navy, was "set up in the Marine Park as a historical relic of the War."

In 1923, during an event celebrating the 300th anniversary of the establishment of Cape Ann, the hull of Lingard's famous flying boat was paraded through Gloucester, but strangely, sometime after the festivities concluded, the iconic hull disappeared. Years later, the rusting hull was rumored to have been housed in a local garage. It remained there for years, the storage fee reportedly being paid for by Olga.

In 1945, the garage that housed the hull was sold. The new owners, anxious to create additional space and perhaps unaware of the dilapidated hull's historical significance, made plans to destroy it. Despite the best efforts of some in the community to save the hull, regrettably, it was burned. "I

Soldiers Memorial Wood. *Courtesy of E.J. Lefavour.*

looked mournfully at a boat-shaped pattern of blackened fastenings on the ground below where the twenty-eight-foot wood-and-fabric hull had been burned," recalled a witness decades later. "I suppose I should have picked up the rivets and [preserved them]." It was a sad end for an artifact that was intended to be placed on display for generations to see.

After the Second World War, Olga spent her free time penning a book about her brother. However, in 1964, a fire ripped through Olga's home and destroyed nearly everything, including her notes. Six years later, in 1970, Olga passed away. Having never married or had children, the Lingard family line ended there.

Before she died, Olga had a memorial constructed in the woods below the former Lingard estate, The Pines, in honor of her brother's sacrifice. In addition to Lingard, the names of two other members of the Gloucester community who died while serving in the First World War were added to the marker.

The memorial, which can still be visited today, is simple—a metal plaque affixed to a rock—but effective nonetheless. It reads:

*ANNISQUAM
SOLDIERS MEMORIAL WOOD
IN GRATEFUL REMEMBRANCE OF
JOHN ERNEST GOSSOM
ERIC LINGARD
BERTRAM WILLIAMS
WHO GAVE THEIR LIVES FOR THEIR COUNTRY IN THE
WORLD WAR*

It is to Eric Lingard—a man with no kin, forgotten to history—that this book is dedicated.

# EPILOGUE

What follows is what happened to the ships, buildings and a select number of participants from this story.

## The Ships and the Buildings

After the Attack on Orleans, the *Perth Amboy* was salvaged and repaired under a new name—the *Nancy Moran*. Much to Germany's chagrin, during World War II, the ship was given to England under the Lend-Lease Act and later participated in the evacuation of Dunkirk. The tug survived the war, but on May 31, 1946, she collided with a tanker in the English Channel and sank.

Although badly damaged, the barge *Lansford*, which once doubled as the Ainsleigh's home, was salvaged after the Attack on Orleans. The other three barges—*766*, *703* and *740*—still rest on the ocean floor. Today, they are frequented by scuba divers.

The USS *San Diego* is also a popular wreck for scuba divers. It is listed in the National Register of Historic Places.

"THIS STATION CLOSED PER COMMANDANT'S PREVIOUS INSTRUCTIONS," written on December 31, 1922, was the last entry made in Chatham Naval Air Station's logbook, a result of the military's effort to downsize after the war. Over time, the station's buildings were torn down or abandoned, left to the elements. In the 1950s, developers bought the forty-acre tract of land, and today the area is composed of seaside homes.

Station Number 40, in Orleans, remained active off and on until World War II. The land on which the station stood changed hands a number of times before eventually ending up under the jurisdiction of the National Park Service. The building itself is long gone, and there is no trace of it whatsoever today.

## THE SURFMEN

Captain Robert Pierce, the keeper at Station Number 40, served thirty-four years in the United States Life-Saving Service before he retired in 1923. He died in 1944 at the age of seventy-nine at his home on Cape Cod.

William Moore, the number one surfman at Station Number 40, became the keeper at New York's Fort Tilden. Moore died suddenly in 1930. He was just forty-eight years old.

Reuben Hopkins left the U.S. Coast Guard several years after the end of World War I and became one of the first electricians in Orleans. Hopkins went on to have three children and retired in 1965. In 1974, he died at the age of seventy-nine while clamming on the flats off Orleans, close to where Station Number 40 once stood.

## THE PILOTS

Philip B. Eaton, the commander of the Chatham Naval Air Station, was relieved of command shortly after the end of the war and transferred back to the U.S. Coast Guard. In 1942, Eaton was credited with saving a number of lives when a train from the B&O line derailed in Dickerson, Maryland. He retired as a rear admiral on August 31, 1946.

Elijah E. Williams, the executive officer at the Chatham Naval Air Station, became a chief engineer with the Munson steamship line after the war. He died in 1948 at the age of sixty-one.

Edward H. Howard, the mechanic who dropped the bomb on the *U-156*, became something of an expert with Liberty motors and would later fly with pilots from every naval air station on the Atlantic Coast. In 1919, Howard was assigned to take part in the first transatlantic flight, but a few hours before takeoff, he got too close to a moving plane propeller; the oak blade neatly chopped off his left hand at the wrist. "I'm all right, sir," Howard shouted to the commander after the accident. "I hope there is bad weather for two weeks, for if there is I'll make the trip with you yet!"

## The Sailors

Captain James Tapley continued to captain tugboats.

After numerous surgeries and trips to the hospital, the injured helmsman, John Bogovich, kept his hand. Fellow Austrian John Zitz was rumored to have lived out his years in Texas.

The Ainsleigh family enjoyed brief celebrity status after the Attack on Orleans, but when the excitement died down, Captain Charles Ainsleigh suffered from a nervous breakdown. In the years after the attack, he worked odd jobs to support his family. Charles, the captain's eldest son, died in 1957. Young Jack took his famous American flag on a savings bond drive in Boston after the raid on Cape Cod. He died in 1998 at the age of eighty-nine, possibly the last survivor of the Attack on Orleans.

\*\*\*

Aside from the historical sign that sits atop Nauset Beach, mentioned in the beginning of this book, there are few reminders that the Attack on Orleans ever occurred.

The curious and those who love history can visit the Orleans Historical Society, located just two miles from Nauset Beach. There, patrons can see pieces of metal shrapnel and shells, at least one of which is embedded in a fragment of wood; a small section of the *Perth Amboy*'s wooden pilothouse; an enamel-drinking cup that belonged to one of the barges; and the oar from the lifeboat of *Barge 766*.

Less than five miles up the road, at the Eastham Historical Society's 1869 Schoolhouse Museum, visitors can view a door that once belonged to the *Perth Amboy*. White arrows point out holes inflicted by German shrapnel.

In one of the yards above Nauset Beach, a lump of cement is rumored to entomb the remains of one of the German shells, but it has never been verified. Below, buried somewhere in the sand or in the muck of the nearby marsh, other German shells allegedly sit where they once fell—the only ones to land on American soil during World War I. There they will apparently rest in perpetuity.

115

# EPILOGUE

***

When writing about a historical event such as the Attack on Orleans, the author is often left to quote only from sources that have been made available to him through research. Unfortunately, not everyone involved in the raid was interviewed afterward by the press. Others did not have the foresight to record their own thoughts and recollections in the years and decades that followed. Thankfully, however, many did, and I am indebted to them for doing so. Although they were not mentioned in the preceding text, I feel it is important to at least note all of the participants who were aboard the tug and barges during the Attack on Orleans, as well as all those who came, in some way or another, to their aid.

## The *Perth Amboy*

| | |
|---|---|
| Captain James P. Tapley | Hollis Pettingill |
| John Bogovich | Andre Serre |
| John Vitz | Pascal Soils |
| Frank Beckworth | Toni Yedreschich |
| Wilfred Dickson | George Yurman |
| William Duley | Joseph Yurman |
| Manuel Gomey | Unknown Man |
| Mike Sgaliardich | Unknown Man |

## The Barges

| *Lansford* | *Barge 766* | *Barge 703* | *Barge 740* |
|---|---|---|---|
| Captain Charles Ainsleigh | Captain Henry Robe | Captain Peter B. Peterson | Captain Joseph Perry |
| Mrs. Ainsleigh (wife) | Captain Robe's wife | Captain Peterson's wife | Virginia Perry (wife) |
| Charles D. Ainsleigh (son) | unknown man | Captain Peterson's daughter | Minnie Perry (daughter) |
| Jack Ainsleigh (son) | unknown man | unknown man | John Leighton (nephew) |
| Rex (dog) | | | |
| unnamed hen | | | |

## U.S. Coast Guard Station Number 40—Orleans, MA
Captain Robert F. Pierce (keeper)
William D. Moore (number one surfman)
Reuben Hopkins (signalman in watchtower)
Elroy Penniman
Allen Gill
Elmore Kenrick
Ralph Cook
George W. Bowley (superintendent located in Provincetown)

## Chatham Naval Air Station
Captain Philip B. Eaton (commander, R-9 pilot)
Lieutenant (JG) Elijah E. Williams (executive officer)
Ensign Eric A. Lingard (HS-1L 1695 pilot)
Ensign Edward M. Shields (HS-1L 1695 assistant pilot)
Chief Special Mechanic Edward H. Howard (HS-1L 1695 observer)
Ensign Thomas Durfee (pilot of HS-1L 1693, which failed to take off
due to spark plug problems)
Ensign Frederick Hicks (HS-1L 1693 assistant pilot)
Petty Officer Cleary (HS-1L 1693 observer)
Ensign Waldo Brown (R-9 pilot who dropped a bomb on a reported
"periscope" at noon)

## U.S. Navy
Josephus Daniels (secretary of the navy)
Franklin D. Roosevelt (assistant secretary of the navy)
Rear Admiral William S. Sims (commander of U.S. Naval forces
operating in European waters)
Rear Admiral Spencer S. Wood (commandant of the First Naval District
in Boston)

# BIBLIOGRAPHY

## BOOKS

Barbo, Theresa. *True Accounts of Yankee Ingenuity and Grit from the Cape Cod Voice.* Charleston, SC: The History Press, 2007.

Berger, Josef. *In Great Waters: The Story of the Portuguese Fishermen.* New York: Macmillan Company, 1941.

Bowers, Peter M. *Curtiss Aircraft, 1907–1947.* London: Putnam, 1979.

Buckley, Joseph D. *Wings over Cape Cod: The Chatham Naval Air Station, 1917–1922.* Orleans, MA: Lower Cape Publishing, 2000.

Burns, Benjamin J. *The Flying Firsts of Walter Hinton: From the 1919 Transatlantic Flight to the Arctic to the Amazon.* Jefferson, NC: McFarland, 2012.

Clark, William Bell. *When the U-Boats Came to America.* New York: Little, Brown, and Company, 1929.

Crisp, Richard O. *A History of the United States Coast Guard in the World War.* Washington, D.C.: Government Printing Office, 1922.

Dalton, J.W. *Life Savers of Cape Cod.* Cape Cod, MA: On Cape Publications, 1991.

Ericson, Peter. *The Kaiser Strikes America.* N.p.: self-published, 2008.

Feuer, A.B. *The U.S. Navy in World War I: Combat at Sea and in the Air.* Santa Barbara, CA: Praeger, 1999.

Gray, Edwyn A. *The U-Boat War, 1914–1918.* N.p.: Leo Cooper, 1994.

Halpern, Paul G. *A Naval History of World War I.* London: Routledge, 1995.

Heller, Adele. *Time and the Town: A Provincetown Chronicle.* New Brunswick, NJ: Rutgers University Press, 1991.

Howe, M.A. DeWolfe. *Memoirs of the Harvard Dead in the War Against Germany.* Vol. 5. Cambridge, MA: Harvard University Press, 1924, 201.

# BIBLIOGRAPHY

James, Henry. *German Subs in Yankee Waters*. New York: Gotham House, 1940.

Keatts, Henry C., and George C. Farr. *Warships (Dive into History)*. Penzance, UK: Periscope Publishing, 2007.

Larzelere, Alex. *The Coast Guard in World War I: An Untold Story*. Annapolis, MD: U.S. Naval Institute Press, 2003.

Paine, Ralph D. *The First Yale Unit: A Story of Naval Aviation, 1916–1919*. Boston: Riverside Press, 1925.

Pearcy, Arthur. *U.S. Coast Guard Aircraft Since 1916*. Annapolis, MD: U.S. Naval Institute Press, 1991, 152–54.

Pletcher, Larry B. *Massachusetts Disasters: True Stories of Tragedy and Survival*. Guilford, CT: Morris Book Publishing, 2006.

Pringle, James R., ed. *The Book of the Three Hundredth Anniversary Observance of the Foundation of the Massachusetts Bay Colony at Cape Ann in 1623 and the Incorporation of Gloucester as a City*. Gloucester, MA: Publications Board of the Three Hundredth Anniversary Executive Committee, 1924.

Putnam, Eben. *Report on the Commission on Massachusetts' Part in the World War*. Boston: Commonwealth of Massachusetts, 1931.

Quinn, William P. *Orleans: A Small Cape Cod Town with an Extraordinary History*. Orleans, MA: Lower Cape Publishing, 2012.

Sims, William. *The Victory at Sea*. London: John Murray, 1920.

Swanborough, Gordon, and Peter M. Bowers. *United States Navy Aircraft Since 1911*. Annapolis, MD: U.S. Naval Institute Press, 1990, 125–27.

Thayer, Lydia Prescott. *Annisquam (Peaceful Harbor)*. Gloucester, MA: Cape Ann Ticket and Label Co., 1994.

Thomas, Lowell. *Raiders of the Deep*. New York: Doubleday, Doran & Company, 1928.

United States Office of Naval Records and Library. *German Submarine Activities on the Atlantic Coast of the United States and Canada*. Washington, D.C.: Government Printing Office, 1920.

Van Wyen, Adrian O. *U.S. Naval Aviation in World War I*. Washington, D.C.: Office of the Chief of Naval Operations, 1969.

Williamson, Gordon. *U-Boats of the Kaiser's Navy*. New York: Vanguard, 2002.

# PERIODICALS

*Barnstable Patriot*, February 24, 1919.

*Boston American*. "American Coast Is Attacked for First Time in Century." July 22, 1918.

———. "Two Wounded as Shell Hits Tug." July 22, 1918.

*Boston Daily Globe*. "German Submarine Sinks Three Barges." July 22, 1918.

———. "Raider Eludes Naval Patrols." July 23, 1918.

————. "Watched U-Boat from Piazza." July 22, 1918.

*Boston Post*. "Shelled by Submarine off Coast of Cape." July 22, 1918.

Brooks, Stewart S. "Orleans Scenes." *Cape Codder*, July 18, 1968.

*Cape Ann Shore*, July 31, 1920.

*Cape Code Times*. "Eyewitness Account Recalls World War I U-Boat Strike off Orleans Coast." July 16, 2000.

————. July 22, 2006.

*Gloucester Daily Times*. "Miss Olga Lingard, Prominent in 'Squam.'" August 18, 1970.

————. "Mrs. Adele R. Lingard Has Passed On." January 27, 1915.

*Harwich Independent*, October 31, 1917.

*Hyannis Patriot*, August, 5, 1918, 2.

————. July 29, 1918, 2.

Koehler, Margaret H. "That Was Some Whale." *The Packet*, July 9, 1978.

————. "The Day the Sub Shelled Cape Cod." *Cape Cod Compass* (1976).

Lombardo, Daniel. "Jack, Rex & the Submarine Attack of Orleans." *Cape Cod Life* (July 2005).

Maloney, Richard C. "When U-Boats Fought Off Cape Shores." *Sunday Standard Times*, July 20, 1958.

Merrill, James M. "Submarine Scare, 1918." *Military Affairs* 17, no. 4 (Winter 1953): 181–90.

Mros, Richard. "Attack on Orleans." *Cape Cod Life* (April/May 1987), 38–45.

*New York Times*. "May Be More U-boat Victims." July 21, 1918.

————. "*San Diego*'s Crew Differ as to Sinking." July 21, 1918.

————. "The *San Diego*, Sunk off Long Island." July 20, 1918.

————. "Stood at the Wheel When Shell Hit His Arm." July 22, 1918.

————. "U-boat Gives No Warning." July 21, 1918.

*Philadelphia Public Ledger*. June 5, 1918.

Scudder, Charles L., MD, and Francis J. Callanan, MD. "The Reconstruction of a German Shell Shattered Arm: The Report of an Historically Important Case." *Boston Medical and Surgical Journal* (September 14, 1919).

Shull, Edward Rowe. "Cape Cod Under Fire." *Boston Herald*, November 28, 1974.

Snowdon, Carol. "The Shelling of Cape Cod." *Cape Codder*, July 19, 1988.

Starr, Joyce. "U-boat Shelled Tug, Sank Four Barges in World War I." *Cape Cod Times*, May 26, 1985.

*The [Baltimore] Sun*. "World War Shelling of Cape Cod Recalled." October 15, 1939.

*Sunday Standard Times*, July 21, 1968.

Vanderbilt, Arthur. "The Two Year Defense." *Cape Cod Compass* (1986).

# BIBLIOGRAPHY

## LETTERS

Gibbs, Herbert R. Personal letter to Russell Gibbs, July 21, 1918. Orleans Historical Society, Orleans, MA.

Tapley, Captain James. Letter to Brooksville Historical Society, May 16, 1936. In *Traditions and Records of Brooksville, Maine*. Brooksville, ME: Brooksville Historical Society, 1936, 114–17.

## WEBSITES

National Park Service. "The Guide's Guide to Cape Cod National Seashore." http://www.nps.gov/caco/planyourvisit/the-guides-guide-to-cape-cod-national-seashore.htm.

———. "Life Savers." http://www.nps.gov/caco/historyculture/life-savers.htm.

———. "Old Harbor Life-Saving Station Historic Furnishing Reports." http://www.nps.gov/caco/historyculture/old-habor-life-saving-station-historic-funrishings-reports.htm.

———. "Shipwrecks." http://www.nps.gov/caco/historyculture/shipwrecks.htm.

UBoat.net. "Type U-151." http://uboat.net/wwi/types/?type=U+151.

U.S. Coast Guard. "A Chronological History of Coast Guard Aviation: The Early Years, 1915–1938." http://www.uscg.mil/history/webaircraft/CGAviationHistory1916_1938.pdf.

———. "Curtiss HS-2L Flying-Boat." www.uscg.mil/history/webaircraft/curtisshs2l.pdf.

———. "Station: Orleans, Massachusetts." http://www.uscg.mil/history/stations/orleans.pdf.

U.S. Navy. "The History of Naval Aviator and Naval Aviation Pilot Designations and Numbers, the Training of Naval Aviators and the Number Trained Designated." http://www.history.navy.mil/avh-1910/APP01.PDF.

## INTERVIEWS

Barnard, Ruth. "Eyewitnesses Recall Submarine Attack off Orleans." Interview by E. Lohr, park historian, Cape Cod National Seashore, Orleans, MA. Audio recording. July 14, 1968.

Berger, Doris, Fisk Rollins, Lewis Delano, Warren Darling and Bill Quinn. Interview about the U-boat attack of 1918 by Orleans Historical Society (OHS Transcripts #003). Orleans, MA. Tape recording. December 13, 1981.

Bonnell, Richard. Interview by Orleans Historical Society (OHS Transcripts #006). Orleans, MA. Tape recording. November 11, 1996.

# BIBLIOGRAPHY

Gould, Vera, and Herbert Gould. Interview by Bonnie Snow (OHS Transcripts #047). Orleans, MA. Tape recording. February 13, 1989.

Hopkins, Reuben. "Eyewitnesses Recall Submarine Attack off Orleans." Interview by E. Lohr, park historian, Cape Cod National Seashore, Orleans, MA. Audio recording. July 14, 1968.

Orleans Historical Commission. "The World War—Held at Orleans Woman's Club." May 3, 1939.

Owen, Aileen Young. Interview by Rod McCall/Orleans Historical Society (OHS Transcripts #023). Orleans, MA. Tape recording. July 28, 1995.

Taylor, Marion Chase. Interview by Orleans Historical Society (OHS Transcripts #040). Orleans, MA. Tape recording. April 26, 1996.

## UNPUBLISHED MATERIAL

Harvard College Class of 1913. "Secretary's Third Report." June 1920.

"History of the U.S. Naval Air Station, Chatham, Mass." National Archives, Washington, D.C., Record Group 45, Box 704, Folder 3.

Howe, Reginald Heber. "Middlesex School in the War." 1921.

Lacouture, Captain John (USN-Retired). "NAS Chatham."

# INDEX

# ABOUT THE AUTHOR

J ake Klim was born and raised on Cape Cod, Massachusetts, just twenty miles from the village of Orleans. As a child, he read snippets about the Attack on Orleans in local periodicals but always wanted to know the full story. Thus began a lifelong fascination with American history.

Klim studied film and video at the University of Maryland–Baltimore County (UMBC), where he also ran cross-country and track. Today, he is a television producer and writer based in North Bethesda, Maryland, outside Washington, D.C. He has worked on productions for the History Channel, the Military Channel, the National Geographic Channel, Nat Geo WILD, the Weather Channel and Animal Planet, among many others. He is also a competitive runner and trains with the Georgetown Running Club in Washington, D.C.